T0098837

The Couple's ROAD TRIP GUIDE

The Couple's
ROAD TRIP GUIDE

*Relationship Lessons
Learned From
LIFE on the Road*

Josh & Aminda
PARAFINIK

New York

The Couple's ROAD TRIP GUIDE

Relationship Lessons Learned From LIFE on the Road

© 2015 Josh & Aminda **PARAFINIK**.

All rights reserved. No portion of this book may be reproduced, stored in a retrieval system, or transmitted in any form or by any means—electronic, mechanical, photocopy, recording, scanning, or other—except for brief quotations in critical reviews or articles, without the prior written permission of the publisher.

Published in New York, New York, by Morgan James Publishing. Morgan James and The Entrepreneurial Publisher are trademarks of Morgan James, LLC.
www.MorganJamesPublishing.com

The Morgan James Speakers Group can bring authors to your live event. For more information or to book an event visit The Morgan James Speakers Group at
www.TheMorganJamesSpeakersGroup.com.

All scripture quotations, unless otherwise indicated, are taken from the New King James Version®. Copyright ©1982 by Thomas Nelson, Inc. Used by permission.

Scripture quotations marked (NIV) are taken from the Holy Bible, New International Version®, NIV®. Copyright © 1973, 1978, 1984, 2011 by Biblica, Inc.™ Used by permission of Zondervan. All rights reserved worldwide. www.zondervan.com The "NIV" and "New International Version" are trademarks registered in the United States Patent and Trademark Office by Biblica, Inc.™

Scripture quotations marked (AMP) are taken from the Amplified Bible, Copyright © 1954, 1958, 1962, 1964, 1965, 1987 by The Lockman Foundation. Used by permission.

A free eBook edition is available with the purchase of this print book.

ISBN 978-1-63047-462-1 paperback
ISBN 978-1-63047-463-8 eBook
Library of Congress Control Number:
2014918262

Cover Design by:
Rachel Lopez
www.r2cdesign.com

CLEARLY PRINT YOUR NAME ABOVE IN UPPER CASE

Instructions to claim your free eBook edition:
1. Download the BitLit app for Android or iOS
2. Write your name in **UPPER CASE** on the line
3. Use the BitLit app to submit a photo
4. Download your eBook to any device

Interior Design by:
Bonnie Bushman
bonnie@caboodlegraphics.com

In an effort to support local communities and raise awareness and funds, Morgan James Publishing donates a percentage of all book sales for the life of each book to Habitat for Humanity Peninsula and Greater Williamsburg.

Get involved today, visit
www.MorganJamesBuilds.com

Habitat for Humanity®
Peninsula and
Greater Williamsburg
Building Partner

CONTENTS

INTRODUCTION

"Americans have found the healing of God in a variety of things, the most pleasant of which is probably automobile drives."
— **William Saroyan**, *Short Drive, Sweet Chariot*

Ah, the allure of the open road. Songs have been sung about it, movies have been made about it. The freedom of driving, the excitement of a new destination—accompanied by favorite snacks and carefully planned music. As hours and scenery fly by, a road trip can become a true bonding experience with the person in the adjacent seat. Ideally, the bond solidifies over games and laughs rather than disagreements and stony silences, especially if the person next to you is your spouse.

My husband and I (Aminda) love the open road, and we love to explore. We started road tripping about the same time we started dating, and we have been traveling ever since—from our home in Phoenix to the beaches of California, the mountains of Colorado or the canyons of southern Utah. On our way back from every fun-filled long weekend, we dreamed of taking extended time off for a Big Kahuna trip, one that would let us relax and really cover some ground.

We believed that God would bless such a trip—He tells us He "will send his angel with you and make your journey a success" (Genesis 24:40)—and he did. Three years after our wedding, we made it happen. We embarked on a three-month-long road trip around the western United States—two people, one truck, 90 days. Through it all, God revealed invaluable lessons about each other and our marriage.

Yes, we were free from the daily grind of our jobs and our house, but we still faced all the challenges that couples do on a daily basis. We had a budget to follow, decisions to make and setbacks to overcome. We were constantly reevaluating our itinerary and budget. Sometimes it was unclear if our car was going to keep moving forward or if the best thing for our relationship was to go backward. Yes, they were simple questions—nothing extreme—but the way we deal with them could have had long-term consequences. Any challenge can create conflict, and if not handled well, conflict can breed resentment and strife, so to ensure the ordinary trials didn't become extraordinary negativity, we ramped up our communication and cooperation.

Road Trip Defined

What was it that we were so excited about doing on our trip? To frame some of the stories and analogies we use, we need to start by explaining that the primary goal for our Big Kahuna road trip was to explore the best rock climbing that the western states have to offer.

This sport, this shared passion, has played a huge role in our relationship since we met on a rock-climbing outing organized by the local Arizona chapter of a national Christian climbing group. Most rock climbers have a special relationship with their climbing partners. After all, partners may literally hold each other's lives in their hands as they hold the end of the rope. A bond forms quickly during such activities. Good communication and trust are critical to the relationship between climbers, so both were fundamental in our relationship even before it became romantic.

While rock climbing has motivated us to explore the country, Josh and I share much more than the mutual enjoyment of a singular sport. We share an enthusiasm for new experiences and adventure, especially out in the world's wonderful wide open spaces, and we both love fresh air, scenic vistas and hidden, tranquil spots.

Our second goal was to escape a Phoenix summer. Living in Phoenix in the summer is tough for two people who like to be outside as much as we do. The call of lush forests and alpine lakes is strong when the world outside your door is dry, brown and blazing hot. Once out of Arizona, we drove straight for the cool, forested hills of northern California, Oregon, Idaho and Colorado.

As much as we love outdoor recreation, we don't want this to define us as full-on adrenaline junkies. Just because we aren't limited by a fear of heights doesn't mean we don't struggle with other fears like anyone else. (We address the benefits of overcoming fear in a future chapter.)

We can't deny the inherent risk to climbing, but there are also plenty of ways to mitigate that risk, which we practice. The more you understand the sport and how the gear works, the less intimidating it becomes. We're both cautious and committed to staying safe. The sport of rock climbing is more than just hanging out in high places. It is a challenging physical activity requiring full body strength, power and endurance as well as mental focus. With many variations of techniques and terrain to climb, the sport provides endless ways to learn and challenge oneself. Not to mention, it's a sport that can take you to beautiful places not many people get to see!

Making It Happen

Even though this book shares many challenges we had along the way, those were not the events that defined our experience. It really did turn out to be our dream trip. We reminisce about it very fondly and have every intention of doing it again! At this point you may be wondering how we planned our life to allow this experience (no, we're not both teachers). Know that it wasn't just a spontaneous whim. Even though we kept our expenses down by packing everything into a fuel efficient pickup and tent camping, it still took a couple years' preparation and commitment. Anyone can travel like this if they set their mind to it. Who knows?—it could be just what your marriage or family needs. Getting out of our routine and comfort zone can expose a lot of relationship flaws like communication issues. But a relaxed environment, like a road trip, provides a safe environment in which to deal with those issues.

Just as it took dedicated effort to move our trip from dream to reality, a fulfilling marriage takes time and dedication. We didn't just sit around and hope that the stars would align or that God would just unexpectedly bless us with the means to make this trip happen. Rather, we took action years in advance, like saving money and career planning. Then God blessed those actions by opening the doors needed for our plans to unfold. It's the same in all aspects of life. If we want something, we need to set our minds to achieving it. So if we want more excitement out of marriage, we need to figure out what "excitement" looks like and start making plans.

A road trip doesn't require climbing, of course. Maybe you dream of touring historic sites or famous eateries. In any case, marriage certainly makes the journey more exciting, rewarding and fulfilling. It's a blessing to have someone with whom to collaborate and cooperate. It feels good to have a partner with whom to discuss life's challenges and take on the curveballs.

Thank you for joining us on our journey about travel, adventure and about marriage. We embarked on both marriage and road-tripping, armed with the wisdom and insight of many couples we love. We have been grateful for that advice and look forward to passing it on.

At the end of each chapter, we provide a Marriage Road Map; attainable steps to living out the principles discussed. We encourage you to answer the questions and follow the steps to keeping your marriage on the road to success.

CHAPTER 1

FUEL UP

*Inject high-performance
positive thinking into your marriage*

So, we're on this vacation that we've been planning for, dreaming of and talking about for years. It's finally here. We pull out of the driveway, and we're completely free to do what we want and go where we please. But first we have to put the hot Sonoran Desert far behind us, so there we are: two people in a car for eight hours. A team of two can accomplish a lot on the job in eight hours, but in a car it's different. Eventually the conversation lags, and all that's left to do is listen to the radio, stare out the window and just ... think.

Josh and I (Aminda) had a lot of leisure time during our trip— many hours sitting in the car, hanging out at campsites and taking long hikes—and all that quiet time was fodder for wandering minds. We each had only one other person on whom to focus our attention, and sometimes we started to think things like "Gee, his breathing sounds loud and raspy in the still of the night here in our tent," or "Golly, that mole on her neck is pretty uuuug-LY."

The dangerous side of a wandering mind is that its aimless thinking so easily manifests itself as words. After thirty consecutive nights together in a tent, listening, it's hard to restrain oneself from blurting out, "Honey, could you just stop breathing? It's driving me nuts!"

During one stop of our trip, it was particularly challenging to maintain positive thoughts. We had just arrived in Wyoming after an awesome week mountain biking in Idaho. It had been a long, tiring drive, but when we woke up the next morning in a grassy, aspen-filled campsite in the shadow of the Grand Teton Mountains, the day looked bright. All we needed was a big pancake breakfast before we got started, but when I (Aminda) pulled out the groceries, it looked as though Josh had already gotten into the pancake mix—from the bottom of the bag. Hmmm, strange. And did he take a bite out of a few cookies, too?

"Uh, Babe, that wasn't me."

"So, how did the hole get there?"

"I think it was a mouse."

"A mouse?! In our food? In our truck? Yuck! Get rid of it!"

Josh had already woken up feeling a little under the weather, and this rodent invasion was definitely making me feel nauseated—and a little grouchy. It was time to go to war. Okay, it was time for *Josh* to go to war, cleaning everything up and setting out an arsenal of mousetraps. That night we caught a mouse. Victory, hooray! … until we found new nibbles out of our bread. The next day we caught another mouse but found more holes in our cereal box. The battle was getting intense, and we wondered what we were up against. Exactly how many mice were in our truck? Where were they living? What if one jumped out of a hole and ran across our laps while we were driving down the highway?

The disgust of having our food supply violated by dirty rodents was almost more than I could handle. Each day my patience deteriorated and my frustration increased; I wanted those filthy things gone. We were already sharing our little truck with bikes, food, clothes, gear and each other. There was no room for mice.

Josh was fighting off illness, and he just didn't have the patience to deal with my bad attitude. Tension was high, and sustaining a positive attitude was difficult. If we hadn't drawn on what little mental discipline we had, we could easily have annoyed each other to the point where we turned the truck around and drove straight back to Arizona.

Private Thoughts Produce Public Behavior

Those frustrations didn't ruin our trip because we had set off with a commitment to a positive attitude. We had invested too much time and preparation into making this trip happen, and we were going to enjoy ourselves, dang it. Bring on the mice, the mosquitoes and the car trouble. We knew we may encounter anything and we were going to get through it all.

The right mindset is at the core of any healthy relationship, even though our thoughts are private. We may think the stuff we keep inside our heads doesn't affect anyone else… until those thoughts spawn words. Which they do, eventually; words can be viewed as actualized, materialized or realized thoughts, and they are far more powerful than thoughts alone. Words lead to actions, and when repeated often enough, our actions become habits. The process is so gradual and subtle that, unless we pay attention, we don't even realize what we're doing. I may have thought I could pout and grumble and keep my bad attitude all to myself. I may have tried to conceal my thoughts and feelings, but I wouldn't have fooled Josh. Hiding our feelings from the ones we are close to doesn't work, because feelings tend to "leak." Nonverbal cues give us away, and most people trust them more than spoken words. So, learning to keep our thought life in check is the first step to generating positive words and actions that will create the peaceful, loving household we want.

Spending long periods of time in close quarters meant Josh and I quickly picked up on each other's leaked feelings. Words are no longer just words when we have extra time to ponder their context and the tone of voice in which they are said. When we spend hours without distractions to knock us off a path of destructive thinking, our negative thoughts can swell and expand until they become tidal waves of criticism. During extended quiet times like this, it becomes important to own our thoughts, which means taking responsibility for them instead of entertaining them or making excuses for them.

The Bible provides plenty of instruction on how we should and shouldn't think. The "shouldn'ts" are summed up well by the apostle Paul. "The acts of the flesh are obvious: sexual immorality, impurity and debauchery; idolatry and witchcraft; hatred, discord, jealousy, fits of rage, selfish ambition, dissensions, factions, and envy; drunkenness, orgies, and the like" (Galatians 5:19-21 NIV).

Yes, Paul specifically says those are *acts* of the flesh not thoughts. We might even describe some of them as feelings. Either way, his list gives us a pretty clear idea of what topics we don't want floating around in our head. They are not Godly actions *or* ideas, so we need to take responsibility for what we do with them.

What at first seems innocent, like a woman becoming annoyed by her husband's indecisiveness when ordering restaurant food, can escalate over time until her view of him as a slow, dithering man who never seems to finish anything he starts, becomes feelings of hatred. In both good times and bad, we want to guard what we think about our spouses. When times are good, it's easy for a man to get lazy and shrug off a twinge of jealousy when his wife receives a raise or promotion. It's a normal feeling, right? No big deal. Really, he's happy for her. However, if he lets that twinge infiltrate, it can fester. He thinks he's let it go, but all of a sudden that pent up resentment escapes when she has to work late. Unaddressed, festering negativity can escalate a minor disagreement into a major fight.

Choose Your Own Adventure

Because we want our relationships to thrive, we take control of our thoughts. Unchecked, thoughts tend to run wild, flitting in and out of our minds for little or no reason. It's a poor policy to dismiss them or justify them if we didn't invite them, because uncontrolled thoughts originate in our subconscious minds. A subconsciously negative attitude is an accumulation of long-held negative thoughts, but the good news is that it's never too late to reverse that negative mindset. The key to doing it is discipline.

The 1952 bestselling book, *The Power of Positive Thinking,* is a classic study on this subject. Author Norman Vincent Peale writes, "When you expect the best, you release a magnetic force in you which by a law of attraction tends to bring the best to you. But if you expect the worst, you release from your mind the power of repulsion which tends to force the best from you." The book quotes pioneering psychologist William James as saying, "The greatest discovery of my generation is that human beings can alter their lives by altering the attitudes of their mind." Modern experts like Tony Robbins and Joyce Meyer have preached variations of this message on positive thinking. Says Meyer, "You cannot have a positive life and a negative mind. Positive minds full of faith and hope produce positive lives."

The process of changing our thoughts is pretty simple. First, we recognize a negative thought, next we acknowledge that we don't want it to have a place in our minds, and then we replace it with a positive thought. Engaging in the process is a matter of choice.

We can think of selecting our thoughts as a "choose your own adventure" story. Let's say that one morning Josh and I are breaking down camp. I'm packing up the tent and find Josh has left dirty Kleenex scattered all over the place. Gross! At this critical moment, I get to choose my own adventure.

Adventure number one: I'm grouchy, and I just don't care. "I guess it doesn't matter if I'm living in a house or in a tent, I'm always picking up after Josh," I think. "Well, I'm not taking it anymore." I stop what I'm doing and yell over to Josh that he can pick up his own disgusting tissue. The ensuing six hour car ride passes in uncomfortable, angry silence.

Adventure number two: I acknowledge my grouchiness and decide that I don't want to "go there." I look over at Josh, who is checking the brakes and cables on my bike before loading it in the truck. "That's right," I think, "I take care of Josh, and he takes care of me. That's why we're such a great team." We spend the car ride in animated conversation about how much fun we just had and what we are going to do at our next destination.

Recognize Trigger Thoughts

Recognizing negative thoughts seems simple, but negativity can be subtle and appear innocent. The first time I have a thought like "Josh never cleans up after himself," it may not be a big deal. But my mind may run with that, over time adding things like "I'm sick of it, I'm not going to take it any more" that are not going to produce any good in the relationship.

We need to train ourselves to recognize these thoughts that don't seem like a big deal but are actually triggers initiating chain reactions of progressively damaging ideas. A trigger thought may start subtly, seeming like a feeling. We may not feel as good as usual about ourselves or someone else. If the feeling is negative enough to get us feeling down, we are wise to prevent it from getting out of hand.

Fortunately, we have help recognizing potentially damaging negativity. That "sense" of recognition is the voice of the Holy Spirit, which abides in us as Christians. "Do you not know that your body is the temple (the very sanctuary) of the Holy Spirit Who lives within you, Whom you have received [as a Gift] from God?" (1 Cor. 6:19 AMP).

Because He dwells in us, we have received the gifts of the Holy Spirit, which include self-control. This means that we automatically have the discipline we need to quickly recognize when our thoughts have taken a dangerous turn. Those gifts may be readily available but honing our sensitivity to the voice of the Holy Spirit requires time in the Word. The Word quiets our minds and gives us peace. It gives us the power to rebuke negativity and brings to mind a positive replacement.

Once we exercise the discipline to recognize destructive thoughts, we need to acknowledge and deal with them. Acknowledging them does not mean denying or repressing them, nor does it mean that we must berate ourselves for having them. When we experience emotions like pain, sadness or anger, it's okay to let ourselves feel them—we just don't want to wallow in them forever. Negative thoughts only produce more negative thoughts, which eventually become negative behavior, so the faster we exit a negative thought pattern, the better.

Moving Up and On

The Psalms provide a clear example of this process. David experienced plenty of low moments in his life. He didn't deny them or pretend they didn't exist. David was very expressive and transparent about his fears, his anger and his weaknesses, but once he expressed his angst, he quickly replaced his troubled thoughts with words of praise and glory to God.

Psalm 69, for example, is titled "An Urgent Plea for Help in Trouble." The first few verses are pretty dreary, starting with the cry, "Save me, O God! For the waters have come up to my neck. I sink in deep mire, where there is no standing; I have come into deep waters, where the floods overflow me. I am weary with my crying; my throat is dry; my eyes fail while I wait for my God." (Ps.69:1-3) By the end of the chapter, his thoughts have taken a completely different direction: "Hear me, O Lord, for Your lovingkindness is good; turn to me according to the multitude of Your tender mercies… let thy salvation, O God, set me up on high" (Ps. 69:16, 29).

We can do the same thing. Once we are aware of a potentially trouble-making thought, we can remove its power by rebuking it. How do we rebuke bad thoughts? By believing the bad thought has no place in our minds.

In 1 Corinthians 2:12, Paul writes, "Now we have not received the spirit of the world, but the Spirit Who is from God, given to us that we might realize and comprehend and appreciate the gifts bestowed on us by God" (AMP). He continues by pointing out that

> The natural, non-spiritual man does not accept or welcome or admit into his heart the gifts and teachings and revelations of the Spirit of God, for they are folly (meaningless nonsense) to him, and he is incapable of knowing them…. For who has known or understood the mind of the Lord so as to guide and instruct Him and give Him knowledge? But *we have the mind of Christ and do hold the thoughts of His heart.* (1 Cor. 2:14, 16 AMP, emphasis added)

We have the mind of Christ! Each one of us needs to believe that, receive it and know that we are not powerless to control thoughts that seemingly run wild. The enemy may try to make us believe that we can't control our thoughts, but we know otherwise. By the power of Christ, we have the ability to transform negative thinking into love and appreciation.

Set Your Mind on Things From Above

Acknowledging a negative thought and recognizing that it is not from Christ still leaves us with a void. The process of transformation requires one more step: we need to fill that void with a positive thought. This is easiest to do when we have an arsenal of positive thoughts ready and waiting.

Building an arsenal of positive thoughts begins with noticing and appreciating the things you like about your spouse. It might be something small—a wife wears an outfit that she knows her husband likes, or a husband brings home his wife's favorite dessert. Those little things are what you noticed and loved early in your relationship, but over time it's easy to expect them and take them for granted. If you make it a point to keep noticing positive things, you'll never stop appreciating your spouse. And when you do notice something negative, simply make an effort to spin it into a positive. That funny shaped mole becomes an exotic feature that makes her unique.

We can add to the arsenal by reading motivational books or listen to encouraging music and speakers. This helps us put Biblical principle into comfortable, familiar language that is accessible whenever we need it.

The best stockpile of positive thoughts is directly in the Word. We're actually promised that when we walk in the Spirit, the Lord empowers our thinking with love, joy, peace, patience, kindness, goodness, faithfulness, gentleness and self-control (Gal. 5:22).

Making Scripture personal is a powerful strategy, and we can do this by using personal pronouns as we speak scripture out loud. For example, when I (Josh) read Psalm 112:1-4, which says, "Blessed is the man who fears the Lord, who delights greatly in His commandments… he is gracious and full of compassion," I can speak it aloud like this: "I, Josh, am blessed because I fear the Lord and find great delight in God's commands. My wife, Aminda, is gracious and full of compassion." The

Bible doesn't apply only to people who lived 1000 years ago. It is living and current, so we can boldly and confidently believe its words to be true in our lives today.

Seeing the Unseen

We can also form the habit of visualization, which helps us focus our thoughts and energy on what we want instead of what we don't want. If, for example, marital disagreements have been escalating into arguments, we can stop the cycle by visualizing how life would look without discord. We can imagine conversations in which we talk things out peacefully, then compromise and agree. This practice is so empowering because it provides a way to deal with a problem, even with an unwilling partner. We can't control our spouses, but we can control how we react to them. If we react by choosing positive words and actions, we will be blessed.

Carrying the positive reaction further, don't keep that blessing all to yourself. Share it by visualizing your spouse being blessed, too. Imagine them succeeding, using their talents, achieving their goals, and fulfilling their dreams and ambitions. Picture them healthy and free from stress. You can see yourself contributing to their happiness, and dwell on ways to be a blessing to them. To actualize your visualizations, you can think of what you might say to encourage and motivate them to succeed.

When focusing our thoughts on change, it helps to be attentive to how we do it—meaning we're concentrating on the positive. Say, for example, a woman has convinced herself that the reason she and her husband are not interacting more often is that he watches too much football, and her prayers and thoughts are focused on getting him to turn off the TV. Just try to visualize the concept of "football off," without seeing more football! It's impossible. The last thing this wife needs to think more about is football, because thoughts of football focus on what she *doesn't* want. She is actually increasing the frustration and blame that she feels toward her husband, even if her intentions are good.

On the other hand, a man wants to spend more quality time with his wife. With positive expectation he could start praying and believing for involvement in specific activities that they would both enjoy, like going on walks, playing board games or taking a class together. This specific, positive request gives God something real and powerful to bring to fruition. We see better results when we focus less on what we don't want and more on what we do.

Held to a Higher Standard

Plenty of external factors influence the way we think about our spouse. Movies and TV regularly portray dysfunctional relationships in the name of humor. Criticism and sarcasm permeate primetime, and we need to ask ourselves if those are the ideas that we want to bring into our homes. Is our entertainment contributing to positive attitudes about our spouse? Monitoring what we watch doesn't mean that we can't enjoy funny shows; we're big fans of humor. It does mean that we want to be aware of thought patterns that can develop as a result of what we expose ourselves to.

The media isn't the only way that negative attitudes about marriage sneak into our minds. Real people can also be enemies of positive thinking. Unfortunately, even the most well-meaning friends, family members and colleagues can be dangerous influences.

Both men and women often fall into the trap of griping about their spouses as a way of bonding with their peers. All it takes is one frazzled friend grumbling about his or her spouse to set off a chain reaction. Suddenly, everyone in the conversation has a sympathetic, similar story.

Women complain about the messes their husbands make, the projects they never complete, or their inability to follow a shopping list. Before they know it, the girls' gathering has flown by in one big gripe session, and an entire group of women return home with confrontational attitudes toward their completely innocent husbands!

"It's okay," a woman may say. "I just share my feelings and get things off my chest so I can move on," or "I'm just exaggerating. Of course, I think my husband is great." Ladies, be careful with these excuses. Remember how quickly one negative thought sets off a chain reaction of complaints. It's best to be vigilant about guarding your hearts. If you really think your husband is great, then it should be easy to make your marriage even more fulfilling by thinking positively. You'll probably also get more attention from your peers with stories of his thoughtfulness.

Men are just as guilty, even though the process unfolds differently. Let's say a group of guys are out together, and one says that it's time to go home. The protests begin. "Dude, really? You have to go home and take out the trash? You might as well stay here. It's not like you're going to get some. Right, Man?"

This gets the guy thinking. "Yeah, that's right. It does feel like all I'm good for is taking out the trash," and proceeds with a lose-lose train of thought. He either goes home on time, full of resentment, or he stays out later and goes home to a hurt and frustrated wife. Men, if your conversations about your wives drift toward the question, "What has she done for me lately?" your narrow focus can create a mindset that puts women in a box. You're in danger of viewing them as objects, being good only for fulfilling your needs. Guard against imaginary standards which can be fabricated by a troublemaking buddy. Such standards breed negative emotions which can cause you to distance yourself from your wife. Couples in long-lasting marriages brag about each other and show each other love and respect.[1]

Summary

The process of acknowledging our negative thoughts, rebuking them and replacing them is so gradual and subtle that without discipline we don't even know that it's happening. For that reason we vigilantly guard thoughts about our husbands and wives in both happy and challenging times—whether we're enjoying a vacation or struggling to balance the checkbook.

The process of identifying negative thoughts and replacing them with positive thoughts requires discipline. You develop discipline by setting goals. If you need to start small, simply give thanks each day for your husband or wife. Then build on that by envisioning them as blessed and asking for God's blessing upon them.

Like any lifestyle change, changing our thought patterns becomes easier with time. It eventually becomes automatic. Once we decide to do it, we can swat a negative thought away naturally, as though it were an annoying fly buzzing around our heads.

RoadMap for Marriage

Questions for Reflection
1. Do you believe that God empowers you to be in control of your thoughts? If not, do you need to confess this disbelief and trust God for this ability?
2. Can you identify sources of negativity that need to be removed from your life? What steps can you take to remove or distance yourself from those things?

Action Steps
1. Create your own arsenal of positive thoughts. Write out some encouraging scriptures using your spouse's name. Write down some qualities you like about your spouse. Keep these with you, in your phone or in your planner, so they are easy to read regularly.
2. Identify a time during the day when your thoughts are idle (when driving, working out, waiting in line, walking the dog,

etc.). Use that time to channel your mind with positive thoughts about your spouse.

3. The next time you are upset, pay attention to what you are dwelling on and focus on how to transform your thoughts. Mentally rewrite recurring thoughts in a more positive way. For example, "I just don't understand women" becomes "Our differences are what make us such a good team." Or turn "He is so annoying" into "I love his charming and funny character."

4. If you still struggle to rid yourself of negative thoughts after 1-3 above, visualization techniques may help. Visualize negative thoughts disappearing. You might imagine them being plucked out of your hand by a bird who flies into the sunset and disappears from sight. Or imagine yourself taking them out to a baseball diamond, standing at the plate and hitting them so hard they fly out of the ballpark and disappear. Throw them into the ocean and let them be carried away by the waves. Heck, even flush them down the toilet!

CHAPTER 2

KEEP YOUR SPARKPLUGS CLEAN

Generate Positive Words and Actions

Not to state the obvious, but Josh and I spent a lot of time driving while on our road trip. Now, driving is one of those unappreciated skills. Unless you are a racecar driver, good driving skills don't really get any recognition—they are pretty much expected, so it was unlikely that, during all of our time in the car, we would think to complement each other on our crazy good driving skills. It would just feel a little unnatural, you know? "Ooh, honey, nice smooth left turn back there, and I just have to say, you are doing an excellent job at staying only eight miles above the speed limit."

Now, climbing—that's another story. It's easy to complement each other there. In fact, Josh is so positive and encouraging that sometimes it can be downright embarrassing. He is unquestionably the stronger climber in our partnership, usually serving as the lead climber, which is the more challenging and risky role in an ascent. He is quite capable of taking the lead on anything, but he often lets me take the lead so that I can stay in practice. No one would ever know this from talking to Josh, however. In his words, I am way stronger and more capable, even to the point of finishing routes for him when they are beyond his ability.

Okay, so he's not completely lying. There was *one* time he started up a route that I should have been leading in the first place, because it was more suited to my strengths. After Josh found himself puzzled by the opening crux move, the most difficult section of the route, I finished the work. Josh bragged about that day for years, always as if it had happened just last weekend. Even though it happened only one time, he spoke of it as if it happened whenever we went climbing. Anytime I feel insecure about a route, he is always quick to say, "Remember that time you were so strong and brave? You still are." His encouragement is specific and meaningful. Josh gives me more than empty words or a clichéd "you can do it." In moments when I am weak and discouraged, Josh is there with positive encouragement. He can do this because his habit of thinking positively gives him a vast reservoir of encouraging ideas to draw from. Rather than keeping those thoughts to himself, he uses them to empower and encourage others. He uses them to express love in ways more meaningful than just saying "I love you." He actively seeks out ways to express his thoughts through words and actions.

The Perfect Ratio

Once we've taken control of our thought lives, external transformation begins. The next step is to give those thoughts power by expressing them with words and actions. Encouraging words and powerful prayers ultimately produce loving actions and a peaceful home. That's just the type of environment we need to ensure happy thoughts, bringing the process full circle.

Based on nearly forty years of studying marriage and relationships, Dr. John M. Gottman, professor emeritus of psychology and head of The Relationship Research Institute, has found that marriages are much more likely to succeed when couples experience a five to one ratio of positive to negative interactions. Conversely, when the ratio approaches one to one, marriages are more likely to end in divorce. He states that a good marriage must have a rich climate of positivity.[1]

What are positive interactions? They include touching, smiling, giving compliments and laughing. Specific acts are not as important as practicing a positive state of mind. If we practice positive thinking, positive interactions should flow naturally. Change is easier when we focus on transforming our mindsets rather than our behavior. Forcing ourselves to perform specific actions can feel unnatural and can be difficult to sustain. A less awkward approach is to look for more outward expressions of the positive emotions we already have. When you feel affectionate, show it. If something makes you appreciate your partner, tell them. If your spouse is happy about something personal, let them share their joys with you. If you form the habit of showing concern, empathy and acceptance, you will see how fast the positive interactions add up.

It's good news that the ideal ratio is five to one and not 1000 to one, and that the occasional screw-up does not doom a marriage. In fact, a certain level of tension and conflict is actually healthy, because couples need to air their grievances, emotions and differences.

Practicing Positivity

If it sometimes feels as though we have more conflict with our spouses than with other people in our lives, it may be because we really do. That close bond may actually foster negativity. How? We communicate effectively with colleagues, service providers and extended family members all day long. Then we come home, and our attitudes shift because we let down our guards and turn off our filters. When we're in public, we think before we talk and say socially acceptable things. A sense of pride keeps us self-controlled so we don't embarrass ourselves. When we come home, we're in our own domains, where we don't have to worry about being polite or worry about embarrassing ourselves. We can let our hair down and relax! We may feel free to say unhealthy things to or about our spouses because the repercussions are not as immediate or obvious. While we don't necessarily want to hurt their feelings, we're not as careful to avoid doing so as we might be in public. That's why we want to keep our thought life in check, so even when our filters are off, we're sowing positive words and interactions into our marriage.

Watching what we say at home doesn't mean we can't be ourselves, can't share how our day went, or can't talk about frustrations, fears and sadness. It simply means that we are vigilant about maintaining boundaries. We're out in the world all day, working hard to hold back negative comments to annoying people. Then we come home and release all that pent up negativity on … uh, our families. But we aren't entitled to yell at our spouses for not setting the table faster just because we didn't get the satisfaction of yelling, "Geez, Grandma, can you drive any faster?" at the slow driver on the way home from work. We can tell our day's stories without making grievances personal by directing our frustrations towards our husbands and wives.

So, no matter what sort of day we have had, we still have to commit to positive interactions with our spouses, and those interactions need to outnumber the negative ones. For every angry "I can't believe you forgot the trash pickup *again*!" there need to be five others: "Have a great day. Thank you for doing the dishes. You are my best friend. That shirt looks great on you. I missed you."

If we come home and have trouble communicating with our spouses, we are most likely letting negative thoughts cloud our judgment and rationale. Regardless of where that negativity is centered, they deserve to have us express ourselves in a healthy, rational way. Developing healthy ways to express negative thoughts is critical, because once negativity has enveloped a marriage, normal interactions become more difficult. A downward spiral develops as each partner reacts defensively, and a focused, committed effort to break the cycle is required.

Clearly, this will be easier if both partners recognize that there is an issue and commit to change. If, however, a spouse is in it alone and faces opposition—if one thinks the marriage could use some change but the other doesn't—commitment to positive thinking has to be stronger. If our spouses react to optimism with sarcasm, we can't engage them. Employing the same filters that we utilize throughout the day will avoid a verbal sparring match that doesn't have a referee. It takes two to fight. When we remove ourselves from a negative interaction, we leave a fighter without an opponent. If we keep at it, a negative spouse will eventually stop trying to fight.

The Marriage Myth

Why does keeping the relationship positive feel like such effort? Unfortunately, the answer might be that we have learned to expect difficulty. Whether from parents, family members, friends or the media, we may hear things like "marriage isn't worth it," or "marriage always fails." The message that marriage is difficult may be influencing your behavior right now.

In our years of marriage, Aminda and I (Josh) have never described marriage as hard or difficult. Have we been told that marriage is or will be challenging? Countless times, and it really bothers us. "You'll find out soon enough," say the veterans. We've even heard pastors and preachers speak in depth about how difficult marriage is.

Come on, now. The Bible says marriage is awesome.

In planning our wedding ceremony, we made a conscious choice not to include the traditional "for better or for worse" lines in our vows.

Our goal was to avoid speaking negativity into the commencement of our union. We didn't want to enter marriage expecting sickness, poverty, or "worse." Instead, we believed for "the better," the blessings and the richness that we would experience together. We exchanged positive vows, because we expected them to have an impact on our words and behavior.

There is a climb in Yosemite National Park called the Nutcracker. Before we climbed it, we read about it extensively in guidebooks and on the internet, and we learned that it required a very difficult move. Even worse, if the lead climber did not stay on the rock through that difficult section, the resulting fall could cause an injury. So, when I approached this difficult move, I had all those messages in my head telling me how tough and scary the section would be, and I spent a lot of time hanging out in one spot and thinking about it. Ultimately, the actual move was not as difficult as my mind had anticipated. Had I simply focused on just completing the move, I could have saved a lot of time and energy that would have been valuable to me on the rest of the route.

It's the same in marriage. Yes, we go through difficult times, and sometimes we disagree with each other. During those disagreements, we sometimes fail to restrain ourselves from saying things we shouldn't. If I blurt out something hurtful or untrue, Aminda is going to react defensively, and a minor disagreement becomes a major challenge. But we don't want to allow the quality of our marriage to be dictated by difficult circumstances, mistakes or our own lack of self-control. If I struggle with self-control or selfishness, meaning that I'm reluctant to give my best behavior, I recognize that this reflects a personal need for better discipline.

His Perfect Partnership
We cannot blame God for bad things that happen. As Christians we know that God is perfect, but we also know that our fallen world is full

of sin. We know that people have free will—they can choose to ignore God and create trouble. Even though marriage was created by God for good, we can exercise selfishness and ignore God's plan for marriage. When we ignore God's plan, we make things more difficult than they need to be.

So, when we feel grumpy or insecure, we need to own up to it and deal with it. We can't blame our marital troubles on our spouses or our marriages. Instead of describing the institution of marriage as difficult, we need to admit that we ourselves might be at fault for marital difficulty. Instead of viewing marriage as the challenge, we can see marital difficulties as the challenges of life—challenges to be faced as a team.

One may argue that a couple can be better prepared for marital trouble if they ready themselves to tolerate it. However, when we mentally psyche ourselves up for battle, we're like boxers throwing warm-up punches before a round. I know that if I go around our house throwing punches, literal or figurative, I create an atmosphere of fear and intimidation, not of peace.

I should clarify that Aminda and I are not completely out of touch with reality. We don't deny that in this fallen world we'll encounter hardships of all kinds. We have insurance coverage to protect us from bad events. We get our regular dental cleanings and physical exams. We don't think that bad things will go away if we pretend that they don't exist, and we don't believe anyone else should, either. We just don't see anything gained by waiting around until we start disliking each other when we can focus our time and energy on enjoying and appreciating each other.

The dating website, eHarmony, posted an article compiling the most common "marriage myths." Included on that list is the myth that "marriage is hard work." "Marriage is lots of work only if you consider sex as work," the article says. "If you consider talking to your spouse as work. If you consider taking a long weekend trips together where you stroll hand in hand, stay up late, and act like young lovers as work. Marriage doesn't need work. Marriage needs attention," it continues. "More often than not, it should feel like play!"[2]

This is exactly the attitude we try to cultivate. Even though we know that life will be challenging, we find no reason to expect it. If we did, we might allow negativity to infiltrate our thoughts, our words, our actions and eventually our lives. Why not make positive declarations? We think marriage is awesome. We love the inside jokes and knowing looks. We love being partners and supporting each other as we fulfill our dreams and goals. We know without a doubt that we have already accomplished more as a team than we could have as individuals, and we know that we'll continue to do so.

Understanding that we are a team, we act like one, nurturing that relationship. We treat each other with respect and consider the other's needs as important as our own. Sure, there are minor annoyances and disagreements, but we both strive to keep them from escalating into battles. Partnership is exactly what makes marriage such a joy and blessing—we don't understand why this should be considered such a burden to bear.

Stay Engaged and Aware

Rock climbing is enjoyable for us. While it's not hard work, it does require teamwork and discipline. A climber's life depends on both disciplined actions and disciplined words. When climbing partners talk to each other from distances of 50 to 200 feet, they can easily misunderstand each other. To prevent accidents and injury in challenging circumstances, a common vocabulary is developed between the belayer (the partner controlling the tautness of the rope) and the other climber. Even when Aminda's faint voice is echoing off a rock from high above, I (Josh) can tell whether she is asking me to make the rope tighter or looser. If she were to change her mind and use a different phrase to express those needs, the consequences could be at least confusing and time consuming, and at worst, deadly.

Just as we have developed the habit of using specific words to communicate, we also follow a familiar series of actions. We have rappelled hundreds of times and can do it almost without thinking, but this familiarity can be dangerous. If we stop thinking, we stop seeing mistakes in the making. To remain alert, we have created mental tricks, like the habit of counting backwards, "3-2-1" as a reminder to double check each of the three components that create a safe rappel.

The same goes for our marriage. Even though I've developed positive habits already, I continue exercising discipline to ensure that I'm not just going through the motions. I want to stay engaged, tuned in to how my behavior affects Aminda, and receptive to whatever form of love she offers.

Maximizing Our Moments

Romans 12:10 commands us to "Love one another with genuine affection, and delight and honor one another." You know your spouse better than just about anyone else on the planet. Think about how awesome that is and how much that empowers you. You know what makes him or her happy, what makes them laugh, what makes them feel good and what encourages them. You are capable of bringing so much joy to your husband or wife that it's almost overwhelming.

One thing that can hinder us from using that power to infuse our spouses with joy is our human tendency to look at everything through the lens of our own world view. Instead of listening closely and paying attention, we make assumptions based on our own preferences.

We all have a "love language," a term popularized by Dr. Gary Chapman and explained in his book *The Five Love Languages*. Some feel love more powerfully when they receive gifts, some when they are touched lovingly, some when they are complimented, some when done a favor, and others when given attention. We tend to show love in the same way we want to receive it, but love will magnify itself when we commit to recognizing our spouse's love languages.

I (Aminda) always appreciate Josh when he remembers little details about places we've been and conversations we've had. It goes a long way in reassuring me that he is listening, caring and engaged. When I try to show Josh love the same way I want him to show me love, I find that Josh may not care how good a listener I am. When I pay attention, I'll realize that Josh is most responsive when I flirt with him or encourage his talents. The power of our positive actions is multiplied when we speak to our spouses in their love language, not our own.

Summary

Marriage doesn't need work. Marriage needs attention. If we meditate on the positive aspects of marriage, our thoughts should manifest as positive actions that make marriage more like play. Positive thinking also maintains the positive climate that is critical to sustained marriage. Knowing that conflict in marriage helps us grow and move forward, we understand that conflict does not define the nature of marriage.

When we are empowered by a positive outlook, we no longer need to blame our spouses or the institution of marriage for marital disagreements. Instead, we recognize that marriage is a team effort, and we take equal responsibility for nurturing the relationship.

Teams don't thrive when all members are exactly the same. No two spouses are the alike in their expressions of love toward one another, their positive actions or their responses to their partners' blessings. We get in sync with our partners, when we stay tuned in to the effects of our behavior and engage fully with them, accepting whatever form of love they offer.

RoadMap for Marriage

Questions for Reflection

1. Do you believe, on some level, that marriage should be difficult? If so, what messages have you heard that have influenced this belief? The next time you hear, think or say "marriage is difficult;" replace it with "marriage needs attention."

2. On some level, do you expect a day to come when you and your spouse start disliking each other? What could you change to become someone whom your spouse will continue to enjoy?

3. How is your ratio? If you took a tally, would your marriage contain five positive interactions for every negative one?

Action Steps

1. Tell your spouse about the times you feel most loved by him or her. Ask him or her to do the same.

2. Take inventory of your daily routines. How to do you act when your spouse leaves for work? When he or she comes home? When the two of you go to bed? Commit to turning these routines into loving interactions.

3. Try some good old-fashioned competition. Keep a tally of the negative and positive (remember, they have to be sincere!) interactions that each of you initiates. Who contributes more to the positive? You could also try some tips from mom, like requiring any put-down to be followed by two compliments, or requiring a quarter deposited in a jar for each impatient reaction (perhaps with the deposits going towards a date of the "winner's choosing, of course).

CHAPTER 3

KNOW YOUR COORDINATES

Keeping Tabs on Your Partner

When we planned our road trip, we knew it was going to be unique and it was going to be awesome. And it was—awesome in its own unique way. It definitely wasn't romantic and relaxing like a honeymoon or a Caribbean cruise.

Our road trip was more about travel than about a vacation. Travel is focused on the itinerary and experiences, while a vacation is focused on rest and relaxation. Our road trip was definitely not a vacation. In fact, it could be downright stressful to arrive in a strange town with only a vague idea about where we would find life's basic necessities, like food and shelter. Only when settled could we unwind and move on to the fun stuff, forgetting our initial anxiety—at least until it was time to pack up again and move to the next town. When we plan a vacation, we usually want to stay in one place, eliminating the potential for stress that comes with every new stop on our itinerary.

There are parallels in romantic relationships. After all, being single can feel like "travel." It's unsettling and insecure not to know how to plan for the future. We wonder if we'll be alone for two more years, ten more, or forever. We feel uncertain about decisions like whether to buy or rent, or whether to take the job transfer or return to school. What effect will those moves have if we suddenly meet the person of our dreams, and he or she is going in a different direction?

When people marry, they might feel as though they're moving from travel mode to vacation mode, and they often anticipate a lifelong honeymoon. While this is a great, positive outlook, here's the deal: marriage doesn't stay in one place. It brings a full itinerary of stops, from purchasing a home to having kids, on to retirement.

Connection and Compromise

Forward momentum requires that you stay engaged. You can't mentally check out and coast through marriage. Because you're traveling as a team, staying engaged means being interested and involved in what the other is going through during each phase of the journey. You want to keep tabs on what your spouse is feeling, thinking and hoping for at any given time. That awareness allows you to support and encourage your partner when needed, keeping issues from escalating.

Early in courtship, couples want nothing more than to talk to each other and to know all about each other. Then they're married, and suddenly all that conversation isn't just talk. What they say isn't simply about who they are as individuals; it is about who they are as a couple, too.

Building a good marriage takes communication and compromise. The compromise required by marriage affects both partners, and often produces a general tendency toward becoming more critical or tuning out completely. Neither is a good strategy for demonstrating care for one another.

Compromise can feel as though we're missing out on something that we really want, which may mean that we don't experience our ideas of what a "perfect" marriage looks like, but it may also mean that we get something better than perfect. How's that? Sometimes we don't really know what we want or need. So, being open to alternatives and compromise can open doors and opportunities that are better than anything we ever imagined or dreamed on our own.

When the initial desire for intimacy fades, married couples have to make a habit of "checking in" with each other. Research has found that couples form more positive emotional connections when they encourage one another's dreams and aspirations.[1] As an added benefit, an understanding of those dreams and goals can aid in decision making and conflict resolution. Discovering those dreams is done by talking to your spouse. You can't be open to your spouse's ideas if you aren't willing to ask about them and listen to them. As you mature in your relationship, you want to keep tabs on how your expectations for marriage are evolving. You have to check in.

We want to know what our spouses expect and hope for in other areas too, like where they'd like to live, work and worship. The better we keep tabs on our partners, the easier it becomes to adjust to their needs. What they want more naturally flows into our own needs, and even though we are still compromising, it feels like less effort. We get more win-win situations than win-lose outcomes. Marriage is all about balance and compromise.

Creating Balance

Figuring out what we wanted from our road trip took a lot of communication, both in advance and along the way. Earlier we shared the story about our rodent invasion, which was one of several instances during the trip in which we had to step back and take an honest look at whether or not we were still having fun. Was there something we needed to change? Did we need to throw in the towel and go home? Conversations during such times are difficult. Nobody wants to be the party pooper or to admit they aren't having fun, but if we don't talk about difficulties, we'll never find balance and harmony.

Balance was one key to our enjoyable travels. While we wanted to experience plenty of new places, we had to pace ourselves. We needed time to decompress when we arrived at each new place. That's how balance looked to us. Other couples define balance differently. Some like to know one place really well while others like to squeeze in as many sights and experiences as possible in a short amount of time. Either way, discovering the right balance is difficult if we don't talk about it and consider each other's needs.

When we were single, we could each move at our own pace, both in life and in travel. We could choose between traveling by bike or by plane. If we wanted to accept an out-of-state job assignment, we could. But we could also decline—it was up to each one of us individually. In marriage, however, finding balance requires us to be in tune with our spouse. We have to listen and be attentive to them before we make decisions.

Attention and Awareness

When our 30-year-old truck stalled outside Yosemite, computers couldn't analyze what was wrong. The mechanics spent their time driving and listening to the truck, being attentive to clues that would diagnose the cause of trouble.

Vehicle design has evolved significantly since that truck was built. Today, cars are run by hundreds of computers. When something goes awry, lights flash and warning messages appear. The driver knows to take the car immediately to the automotive technician, who hooks it up to complex diagnostic equipment, which connects with other computers to identify the problem. The technician knows exactly what to fix, having barely cracked the hood.

Wouldn't it be great if the same were true of our spouses—if warning lights appeared when they got off balance, and all we had to do was hook them up to a computer to find out what was wrong and how to fix it? In reality, we have to respond to them as we would to an older vehicle. Without warning lights and fancy diagnostic equipment, they require a different approach.

To know when there is trouble, we first have to be aware of how the car performs when there *isn't* trouble. We listen to how it sounds and pay attention to how it feels. Drivers of old cars can't tune out while driving. If they ignore unusual noises, the underlying problem can get worse and worse until the vehicle breaks down and leaves them stranded. Instead, they remain attentive to the rhythm of the car, to its unique character. Only then can they notice when something feels "off" and requires further examination. Without computers, diagnosis is a more methodical process of investigation, starting with general observations and ending with a specific diagnosis.

Staying in Sync

We want to be just as attentive in our marriages. As you get to know your spouse, you get in sync with their rhythm. You learn to recognize an unusual reaction or response. If you ignore unusual noises in your car, you risk a breakdown. If you ignore unusual behavior in your spouse, the problem grows and becomes harder to deal with. Instead, when we notice something "off", we can seize the opportunity to diagnose the problem. We do this by letting them know that we sense they aren't fully themselves and being available to talk about it. Diagnosis may not be easy or immediate. A spouse may not fully realize what the source of their trouble is and may rebuff initial inquiries. For example, how often does some variation of this scene happen between husbands and wives?

Husband: "Hey honey, are you OK?"

Wife: "Yeah."

Husband: "Is something wrong?"

Wife: "No."

Husband: "OK. Well, if you need to talk about something, let me know."

Wife: "Why would you say that? I said nothing's wrong."

Husband: "Well, you just seemed a little quiet, a little distracted."

Wife: "What do you mean by that? Do I have to be talking all the time? Seriously, why does something have to be wrong? Why can't I just be quiet? I thought you liked it when I just shut up and let you watch sports? So what do you think we should talk about? Football? Is that all you think about? I hope you didn't say something to your mom. She'll think I'm depressed. She always thinks something wrong with me. Then she'll tell the whole family and they'll all think I'm crazy and I'll get a bunch of Dr. Phil books for Christmas." (Wife bursts into tears.)

Husband: "Honey, are you OK?"

Wife: (still crying) "Yes."

Women, we need to help our husbands help us. Men are natural fixers. When they identify a problem, like "my wife is upset," they want to fix it. We can either tell them what they can do to help fix our moods (e.g., make an ice cream run or give a back massage), or explain that we're feeling emotional and can't be fixed. No matter what, we can always tell our men that they can give us a big hug and just let us cry for a little while. It's really hard for men to stand by helplessly without being able to fix a problem. If we continually rebuff our husbands' efforts to help, they will eventually give up and stop trying.

Gender Generalities

Because women are more apt to sense emotion in others and are good at reading nonverbal signals, they get frustrated when their husbands don't understand cues. This biological difference between men and women is usually enhanced by American upbringing. Girls are often taught that the display of emotion is acceptable, while boys are usually cautioned against it.

Men don't need to get discouraged and give up. Instead, bear in mind that women's emotional awareness also means that they are quicker to spot and deal with troubled spots in the marriage. Men tend to have a rosier view of relationships, which is positive; it just means you want to take care not to brush off your wife's distress, even if the distress seems irrational or overly emotional. The best thing that men can do is to show concern and channel their confusion into prayer for wisdom and understanding.

Gender differences are confusing, but they certainly prevent apathy and keep us on our toes. Once we've been married for a while, we think we know our partners well enough to understand their needs and wants. Then, we go through the motions of doing what we think they want us to do. While we may grow better at understanding our spouses, we can't allow assumptions about them to become an excuse for avoiding communication. Our core personalities may never change, but as we grow and mature, our needs evolve along with us. We have already established that partners receive love in different ways. When we ignore those differences and interpret our spouses' needs through our own lenses, we miss the opportunity to express love in the most meaningful way possible. In the same way, we don't want to get lazy and assume that we know all of their needs.

Reaping the Rewards of Discipline

Regularly checking in with your spouse is just one form of communication. Developing small, interactive habits will help maintain a positive outlook on the future of your marriage and set bigger goals for your relationship, ultimately strengthening the foundation of a faithful union.

Checking in doesn't have to be formal—just timely. Redbook Magazine featured a marriage counselor with 31 years of experience who found that the majority of failing couples she sees have stopped asking each other "How was your day?" It's a simple question, but it conveys compassion. Checking in with your partner daily represents a commitment to nurturing the marriage. When that commitment ends and you stop asking, your partner feels taken for granted, a feeling which quickly degrades and becomes deep resentment. Starting a simple conversation with "How was your day?" is an easy way to sync with your spouse's regular rhythms. You quickly find out what upsets them, what excites them and what makes them bored and restless.[2]

Making the daily check-in a life-long habit takes discipline, and because discipline is such an important component of successful marriage, it is an important character trait. Discipline entails delayed gratification—like taking a couple of minutes to check in with our spouses, even if we would rather be talking to friends or watching TV.

A husband may not feel like asking his wife how her day was. He may think to himself, "My wife drove to work, sent some e-mails, made some phone calls and then drove home. Why do I need to hear that every day?" Or, maybe her unreasonable clients and unsympathetic boss are best left behind at the office. If that's the case, no problem. We can find our own conversation starters. What matters is the habit of connecting and listening.

Just as our thoughts produce words and actions, our actions produce habits, and our habits give structure to our lives. Habits can be behavioral, like looking both ways before crossing the street. They can also be related to our temperaments, like a tendency to see the glass "half full." Our parents endowed us with many of our habits, and in marriage we learn new ones from our spouses. Because we also influence them to form habits, we may need to check-in, to ask them how those habits are positively or negatively affecting our marriages. When that discussion turns to negative habits, it might get more difficult.

Communicate Core Issues

Engaging in tough conversations immediately instead of putting them off takes discipline. In the short term, handling personal challenges might be uncomfortable, but ultimately we'll be happier if we tackle them quickly. If we spend too much time working up the nerve to express our needs, our frustrations build. By the time we finally have the conversation; it is more intense and difficult than it would have been months or years ago.

Talking to your spouse about their quirks, habits and the reasons that they do the things they do may take time as you patiently ask the deep, probing questions required to get to the root of behavior patterns. In the process, you learn more about them, uncovering their hidden needs and desires. When you learn about those needs, you can help fulfill them, and when they are fulfilled, your spouse is happier. When they are happier, you are happier.

You may have to dig a little to unearth the sources of strong positions or opinions within a conflict—both your spouse's and your own. You may have to stop and do some self-reflection, to ask, "What feelings are at the core of my opinion about this issue?" or "What is my past history with that issue?"

Once we understand how a behavior affects our spouses, and once we've rooted out the reasons that we do the things we do, communication becomes smoother. On the other hand, when we understand where our spouses are coming from, it may make their upsetting behavior more tolerable.

Set up for Surprise

Each time a problem is diagnosed and fixed in an older car, we learn from it. The next time we hear the same squeak or rattle, we know where to look first. We become more in tune with the vehicle, but we can't pay less attention to it. As it ages, the car is more prone to disrepair and needs even more care.

In the same way, we can't get complacent in our marriages. We have to stay in tune with the ebb and flow of our spouses. As we age, we make transitions that cause us to take stock of where we are and motivate us to make adjustments. The most infamous example is middle-age, but transitions and adjustments are also triggered by preparing for children, rearing children, seeing children leave the nest, experiencing a career slump or losing a loved one. These are emotional periods that we must work through. If we stay in tune, stay aware during these times, we minimize the risk of encountering "suddenlies." *Suddenly* a husband or wife wants to start their own businesses, go back to school or become a missionary in Zimbabwe. Though these "suddenlies" usually have been incubating for a while, they often feel very sudden to the person who is faced with the revelation. We want to be in tune with our spouses, to know how they feel about where life is taking them. Are they content today and optimistic about the future, or are they a little restless and confused?

My (Josh) skills lean naturally toward leadership and public speaking. While Aminda and I were still dating, I shared a feeling that someday I might be called to utilize my talents as a preacher, or maybe in politics. Aminda didn't nod and absently mindedly think "Oh, that's nice honey." She tucked that bit of information away. Now, every couple of years she'll check in and ask me if I'm feeling lead in that direction. If I say no, she asks if I'm feeling led in another direction. Where do I see myself, career-wise, in five or twenty years? How can I get there and what can she do to help?

Join the Journey

A couple we know had been married a couple of years when the husband confessed for the first time that he had always dreamed of joining the military. So, in his mid-twenties, after completing college and with his wife's support, he joined! Life as a military family is undoubtedly an adventure, and not the one his bride had planned, but she had an open mind and has embraced the resulting lifestyle and travel. Her adventure began because, as a couple, she and her husband were willing to check in with each other, to express their expectations about how they envisioned their future. As a result, their journey has been fulfilling and has given them a network of friends across the country.

All of us—husbands and wives—have the potential of springing a "suddenly" on our partners. We all may have ambitions that we haven't shared. Out of consideration for them, we might want to voice our aspirations sooner rather than later. Sure, we might be embarrassed, or maybe we've convinced ourselves that our desires are just crazy dreams that will never happen. But we should feel safe enough to trust them—even with a "crazy" dream like getting a pilot's license or buying a farm.

Embracing Honesty

By opening up to your spouse and telling him or her you need and want, you are actually increasing your odds of making that positive change happen. When you get your spouse on board earlier rather than later, you give them the opportunity to adapt to an idea or a change. You give them time to see how an idea could become reality, and, you offer a chance to share the dream and become your champion rather than your opponent. The more open and honest you are, the more it helps them understand and embrace your dreams, and the easier it is for you to understand and embrace theirs.

We may need to seek God, to ask for His help to get us in sync with our partners and to understand the sources of their needs. Often, goals represent deeply seeded emotions and values, like security, freedom and excitement. We may find it hard to relate to a spouse's need for something like a flashy new car until we consider that he or she was raised in poverty or deprivation. If we find ourselves resistant to our spouses' dreams, it is wise to consider whether our lack of support originates in the spirit or in the flesh. Are we are afraid to change or to see them change, or is there wisdom in our reluctance?

Romans 8:5 tells us that when we live in accordance with the Spirit, our mind is set on what the Spirit desires. If we are surrendered to living our lives for the glory of the Lord, we can trust that He will show us how to glorify Him by using our unique talents and abilities. We never know when something that seems like a silly fantasy has the potential for helping us fulfill a greater purpose, to open a path to what previously seemed an impossible destination. We can't allow ourselves to ignore or bury our dreams.

Summary

Through the challenges, the ups and the downs, marriage is a team effort. The bond and partnership between husband and wife is unique to the individual couple. We forge these partnerships by becoming aware of what makes us a good team: how we solve problems, enjoy inside jokes, include each other in our daily rituals at home and share visions for our lives together. Our differences, our unique ways of dealing with problems and envisioning the future, bring depth and wisdom to the team.

The differences between men and women can be confusing. We can stay confused, or we can make the effort to understand our spouses. We can't stop getting to know our spouses when we are done dating, simply going through the motions of marriage. Life ebbs and flows, and we go through different seasons and periods of change together. Through it all, we keep expressing our appreciation and gratitude for the lives we are building together. We know that no matter what, our lives will be good, because God promises his servant will prosper and be exalted (Isa. 52:13 AMP).

RoadMap for Marriage

Questions for Reflection

1. Do you have a regular time each day to check-in and connect with your spouse? Do you give him or her full attention during this time?
2. Do you have unexpressed needs or goals that you need to share with your spouse before they become "suddenlies?"

Action Steps

1. If neither of you feels a need for change but has trouble expressing your needs to each other, use these questions as a way to identify and build on strengths and what is already working in your relationship. This process can ward off stagnation, and can aid in implementing positive change.
   - If we don't do anything different, where will we go?
   - What is already working? What makes it work?

2. If you are unsure of how to act on a desire for change, try a technique sometimes called a Gap Analysis. Together, identify:
   - your current state
   - your desired outcome

What indicators will mark your arrival at that desired outcome? What gaps create the different between those two states? What steps do you need to take to fill those gaps?

CHAPTER 4

U-TURNS NOT ALLOWED

Staying in the Present

How many of us can say we've planned a trip that unfolded perfectly? Everything goes just as expected, not a single delay or drop of rain. Doesn't happen, does it? The good thing is that the unexpected often turns out even better than we had hoped—the botched hotel reservation that leads to a weekend in the presidential suite, for example. On those happy occasions, we're usually so excited about our good fortune that we don't think too deeply about how it happened, who was responsible for it or what we could do to increase the chances of it happening again.

On the flip side, when unplanned events are unpleasant, it's easy to focus on exactly those things. We analyze details and point fingers. Aminda and I (Josh) certainly battled those inclinations throughout our road trip, as we encountered plenty of speed bumps along the way. We learned how essential it is to make decisions confidently and then move forward without second-guessing ourselves, because regret can become a cancer in relationships.

Extended life on the road requires a high level of fluidity. We were constantly working to create a balance between structure and flexibility. Some structure is desirable. We had a list of areas we wanted to visit, and we didn't want to miss them because we had been too leisurely. We also needed to plan around holiday weekends when campgrounds would be full. Even so, we kept our itinerary loosely structured, which required plenty of on-the-fly adaptations. Because our activities were so weather-dependent, we needed the flexibility to move toward bluer skies at the next destination.

Keep on Believin'

Sometimes everything would go our way. We would quickly find a beautiful, inexpensive camping area, and the weather would allow a perfect balance of activity and rest. Other times—well, we have plenty of stories about the lessons we learned about patience, flexibility and avoiding regret.

Like the day we drove into Yosemite National Park. Or tried to. The park was one of the first big stops on our itinerary, and our excitement was palpable. Yosemite is a magical place for climbers, offering enough climbing on the towering granite domes to last a lifetime. The park's thundering waterfalls and meandering river create views in every direction. We couldn't wait to catch our first glimpse of the monolith known as El Capitan, which signals one's arrival and keeps a stately watch over the valley below.

We were excited by how well our old truck was climbing the steep, windy mountain pass before descending into the Park. The truck, on the other hand, didn't seem to think it was ready for such a challenge. About

20 miles from our destination, it decided we had pushed it hard enough for the day and needed a break.

We sputtered to the side of the road and popped the hood. I couldn't find a thing wrong. We were going to need help. We were filled with despair as we headed back down the mountain and into the dry high desert of central California. Was this it? Was the truck dead? Was our trip ending right there, when it had barely begun?

Our friendly, toothless tow-truck driver kept us from getting too glum, as he entertained us with funny stories and helped us get settled in his hometown. The next day, while we anxiously awaited news from the mechanic, we made the most of our break from camping— with long hot showers, a full breakfast and lots of cable television. Finally, after an entire day with the truck, the mechanics confessed that they couldn't find anything wrong with it. We weren't entirely sure how to react to the news. We were thrilled, of course, but also skeptical. Could we trust these mechanics? Could the same problem stall us in the same place on the same hill if we continued? We didn't know. What we *did* know was that we only had two directions to travel: forward or backward. Fortunately, we chose to move forward because that was the only car trouble we had all summer.

The whole trip was an exercise in staying in the moment. Sure, we got lost, rained out and delayed, but heck, we weren't sitting in front of a computer at a 9-to-5 office job. We had every reason to believe that each day was going to be great. We never turned around and went back to a place we had already been. We were always moving forward. If we looked back, it was only to talk about how awesome the trip had been so far.

Every Day is a New Day

Staying in the present is a delicate balance between remembering where we've been and looking towards the future. We know that reflecting on the past can be a healthy way to stay positive when we're facing struggles in the present. Remembering God's faithfulness, His answers to prayers and His blessings can give strength and hope for tomorrow. The Lord even gave us the rainbow, so for the rest of man's time on earth he can "...remember the everlasting covenant between God and all living creatures of every kind on the earth." (Gen. 9:16 NIV).

After a summer on the road, we returned to Phoenix in early September. While autumn weather had begun turning cooler in most of the country, September temperatures in Phoenix were still over 100 degrees. This was a shock to our systems after several months in the cool mountains. Instead of complaining about being back in Phoenix, we chose—okay, forced ourselves—to remain thankful for the wonderful months of travel we'd had.

We handled the change by reflecting on those wonderful days we had spent sitting together in silence atop a peak, savoring fresh mountain air while taking in the grandeur of the Rocky Mountain range, stretching across the horizon in every direction, or getting caught in a gentle, misty rain that unleashed the fragrance of the surrounding pine forest as we finished descending a perfect bike trail. Before we knew it, September was over, and we could enjoy another balmy winter in Arizona.

Choose the Best Reflection

Like looking back on a good vacation, reflecting on marriage is healthy. What initially attracted you to your husband or wife? What qualities did you initially admire in them? Celebrating memories of your love and commitment to them will help build your present relationships. Loving memories can help you generate the thoughts needed to maintain a positive climate within marriage.

Dwelling on past disappointments, however, can be dangerous. A husband who can't let go of the way his wife's body looked before kids, for example, sets himself up for never-ending dissatisfaction. Or he may have been a strong, popular athlete in high school who is now grieving that his "glory days" are behind him. Such thoughts need to be kept in check and should be channeled into positive thoughts about staying fit and healthy. Looking back can help us deal with the present, but dwelling on the past prevents forward movement.

Returning to past conflicts can also be a source of trouble. Lamentations 3:22-24 is a beautiful passage reminding us of the beauty of a fresh start that each new day offers.

> It is because of the Lord's mercy and loving-kindness that we are not consumed, because His [tender] compassions fail not. They are new every morning; great and abundant is Your stability and faithfulness. The Lord is my portion or share, says my living being (my inner self); therefore will I hope in Him and wait expectantly for Him. (AMP)

The Lord's compassions are new every morning, and we need to extend the same leniency to our spouses. They deserve a fresh start each day. If we keep any tally of their behavior, we should keep track of how much they bless us. Dwelling on what they failed to do for us yesterday or last week is unhealthy. The Lord focuses on our potential and what we're capable of accomplishing; he doesn't keep a scorecard of what we've done in the past. When we have the same attitude towards our spouses, we give them freedom and confidence.

When we focus on keeping our thoughts positive and in the present, we foster relationships of trust and harmony. If we can't forgive or let go of something, it has to be dealt with so that we can live in the present. This means asking both God and others for forgiveness, and also extending forgiveness to those who have wronged us.

Don't Delay Discussion

So, what if something from the past is truly creating a marital disconnect? The key to connection is not to dwell on the issue, but to deal with it, and to deal with it sooner rather than later. That means initiating a conversation as soon as a spouse feels offended by his or her partner. The conversation should include an opportunity for apology, which leads to forgiveness and closure. On the other side of the coin, a spouse who needs to come clean about something should stop everything and get it off his or her chest immediately. If an important conversation is waiting to be had or a confession to be made, just get it done. Procrastination and excuses do nothing but keep us stuck in the past and make it difficult to live in the present.

When couples don't make time to talk about them, frustrations manifest in unhealthy ways. When a husband or wife has to say, "Honey, I noticed you threw three dishes across the kitchen. Is something wrong?" the couple has waited too long to deal with a difficult issue. Expressing our emotions takes courage, which doesn't grow with time. Choosing to say, "I'm sorry. I feel terrible about this. I need your understanding; I need your forgiveness; I need your support" is the bravest and best way to initiate a difficult exchange.

Check your baggage

Too much baggage on a trip is a burden. Who likes to maneuver five suitcases around the airport, figure out how to organize them in a cramped hotel room and then try to cram everything back into them when they leave? Nobody.

Staying light is an easier way to travel and was critical on our trip. Our truck wasn't getting any bigger, and it was the only space we had. When we were packing for our trip, we followed a simple suggestion from travel experts: we laid out everything we thought we needed or wanted, then put half of it back. Along the way we had to avoid buying or acquiring too much stuff. If the truck got too full, the space was crowded and uncomfortable.

Similarly, we need to lighten the load in our relationships. Our extra baggage—anything from negative thought patterns to inappropriate expectations—only brings dysfunction into the present. If we find ourselves thinking that a disagreement mirrors ones we've had in the past, we don't want to project any past anger, frustration or helplessness into the present situation. Our spouses deserve better than the accumulated garbage we've collected. They deserve our full attention and our open minds.

Through observations of people in your family and relationships, you collect ideas and opinions about all sorts of things. These ideas and opinions can create baggage. When those opinions become too strong, it's easy to project them onto your spouse instead of listening objectively. When you find yourself stubbornly insisting that things have to be done a certain way, you need to do some introspection. Do you hold onto a belief because it is in the best interest of your marriage, or is it an irrelevant belief based on past experience? A healthy marriage requires room for flexibility, compromise and new agreements.

If our husbands or wives are struggling under the burden of old baggage, we have to address the problem. Ephesians 4:15 tells us to "speak the truth with love." When approaching a difficult discussion about old baggage, we will be better received if we enter the conversation not only with our own best interests in mind, but also the best interests of the relationship. Hurts that we carry around become encoded in our minds, and breaking that encoding can take focused and fervent prayer. Dealing with deep burdens and hurts might be best addressed through counseling.

Deciding to Deal

When a spouse's past has interfered with the present, or when a spouse has made a poor decision in the present, forgiveness doesn't always come easily. Mistakes can be major, like a financial investment that soured, or they can be minor, like a poor choice of a birthday present. Either way, we need to deal with the problem, learn from the situation and move on. Regardless of the mistake's severity or outcome, it's important to stay grounded in trust—trust that our spouses have our best interests in mind. Trust that all things work together for good to those who love God (Rom. 8:28).

You have to let go of any belief that your husband or wife is responsible for your happiness and well-being. Your spouse is human, and human beings will let us down. The only one who can truly meet your needs is God. He is the One that gives you peace, strength, joy. When you embrace that, when you truly rely on God for security and happiness, your spouse is liberated from that responsibility.

When intentions are good, resolutions to problems should come easily, but sometimes we're just idiots. When we are, we need to own up to it and give each other closure. Is an apology or explanation needed? Start talking, even though it may not be easy. When you make decisions that negatively affect your spouse, it doesn't feel good. Your self-esteem drops. Your survival instincts may tell you to forget about it and to bury the situation without dealing with it, but you can't. When your spouse makes decisions that cause you to suffer, you may be tempted to let them experience the same suffering, but unresolved conflict only grows bigger. A grudge held against a spouse as punishment for a bad decision grows like cancer, and it must be diagnosed and treated.

Debriefing Decisions

I (Josh) am a team building facilitator by profession, and I have become skilled at overseeing conflict resolution. One of the most effective techniques I use is the "debrief." After every group activity, the team sits down and talks about their observations, what they learned about each other, what they did well and what they didn't do well.

Having seen the success of the technique in difficult situations, I have introduced variations of "the debrief" into our marriage. Aminda and I have discovered that is an effective tool when we're faced with the aftermath of botched decisions. We talk through the decision-making process and try to figure it out. Did we misinterpret information, communicate poorly or fail to research the situation thoroughly? What did we learn and how can we use that insight in the future? This process leads to great communication and teamwork, and it helps us gain insight and wisdom into each other and the way we work together.

The key is to using the process well is to focus on gaining wisdom without getting sucked into the "coulda, shoulda, woulda" syndrome of regret and blame. This is what happens when we focus too narrowly on what we could have done, what we should have done or what we would have done had we known what the future held. It is usually non-productive, because none of us can predict the future. All we can do is work with what we have in the moment and then move on.

Before debriefing, we can establish up front that a bad decision is not a failure. Self-worth does not depend on decision-making skills, and neither husband or wife deserves to pay for whatever mistakes were made. Debriefing is time for learning, not judgment. If done with the right attitude, a good debrief can eliminate regrets and conflict. When something doesn't go our way, we acknowledge that we made the best decision with the information available at the time. We evaluate how we want to deal with the outcome, and the process begins again.

We find a perfect example of debriefing in the Book of Job. Scripture describes Job as an upright and blameless man—a pretty big compliment—but even Job recognized when he needed to repent, without defending himself or making excuses. And boy, did he repent deeply! When the Lord revealed to him that he had spoken rashly and presumptuously of Him, Job responded, "I had heard of You [only] by the hearing of the ear, but now my [spiritual] eye sees You. Therefore I loathe [my words] and abhor myself and repent in dust and ashes" (Job 42:5-6 AMP).

The Lord did not let Job wallow in the ashes of repentance for long. Instead, He sang Job's praises, saying to Job's friends, "My servant Job shall pray for you, for I will accept [his prayer] that I deal not with you after your folly, in that you have not spoken of Me the thing that is right, as My servant Job has" (Job 42:7 AMP).

Let. It. Go.

Job had the humility to admit his shortcomings, the confidence to put them behind him and the meekness to accept the Lord's praise. Some of us struggle to forgive ourselves for mistakes even after our spouses have done so. While self-awareness is positive, self-flagellation is unhealthy.

Within the Christian church is a belief that we are capable of totally screwing up God's plan for our lives if we are not fully attentive to God's guidance every single second of every day and in the smallest decisions. We read that God planned out all of our days before we were even born (Psalm 139:16) and assume the full burden of fulfilling our life plan.

Fortunately, we can rest assured knowing that God is bigger than our mistakes. Of course He wants us to abide in His will for our lives, because He knows that we will have the best lives possible if we do. But He also knows when our hearts are in the right place, He won't let an overdue bill or a forgotten phone call throw us completely off course. We have been given the gift of a Savior who does an amazing job of correcting our mistakes. Instead of living in fear that we are going to screw up, we can live in faith that God's mercies are new every morning.

Look Forward in Faith

In the New Testament, James instructs Christians to ask God for wisdom. The *Maxwell Leadership Bible* summarizes his advice beautifully: "If we do ask God for wisdom, we must ask in faith, expecting His answer. Once [we] gain perspective and trust God for wisdom, the only thing left to do is to anticipate solutions and exude optimism."[1]

Anticipate solutions and exude optimism. How inspiring! How liberating that we can so fully turn our decision making over to God! We ask for wisdom, we believe God for it, and He provides. It's that simple. The apostle Peter is a timeless and inspiring example of a man who didn't let past failures hold him back. Peter denied Christ, but he owned up to it and went on to be an incredible witness. As the *Maxwell Leadership Bible* states, "Effective leaders walk by the power of the Holy Spirit. They realize that all of us, even those with the best of intentions, are prone to failure when we walk in our own strength and not in the empowerment of the Spirit."[2]

Sometimes we forget how much strength we have in God. When we try thinking positively but just can't break through the regrets, temptations and disappointments that consume our thoughts, we can learn from Job's humility by acknowledging that God has transformational power. When we have big problems, we can pray them down until we can find some peace and move on.

The Future's so Bright

The past isn't the only place where people can get stuck. Some of us may have trouble staying in the present because we can't stop thinking about the future. What's wrong with that? Having goals and aspirations is completely positive, but we need to remain grounded in the present. The danger of thinking too much about the future is becoming overly focused on how much better life will be when a certain event takes place. "I'll be happy when I get married or when I have kids" quickly turns into "life will be so great when the kids are out of the house." Instead, why not focus on why life is great *right now?*

Life is happening now. It's moving forward with or without us. If we have a "grass is greener" mentality in which we dwell on how good life would be if we had that house or car or relationship, we'll never fully experience God's peace and joy. We can get so wrapped up in this mindset that we're always waiting for something to happen before we can have fun.

In marriage, you're going to have trouble if you are always waiting for your relationship to be better or for your spouse to meet your needs. Instead, you need to take action, replacing that wishful thinking with optimism about the present. That can only happen when you take control of your thoughts *today*, instead of putting it off until sometime in the future.

The Relationship Zone

So where do we find balance between learning from the past and looking toward the future? To illustrate the answer, we'll use a sports analogy. Athletes in all disciplines have at least one thing in common. They all experience what's commonly known as "the zone," a coveted state of "total concentration and involvement, control, a unity of mind and body and a sense of personal fulfillment at an optimal level of performance."[3] In this state it feels as though difficult skills are completely natural.

Aminda and I know this feeling from climbing. When climbers are in the zone, their minds don't have to provide step-by-step instructions like "put your right foot here, now your left hand there." Rather, their minds and bodies just flow, and the climbers know exactly what to do with the features of the rock in front of them. How does this happen? Through muscle memory, resulting from thousands of hours of practice and training. After climbers have repeated a single move over and over again while focusing on good technique, they can eventually perform it perfectly without thinking about it.

During their training, climbers still experience both successes and failures. Even if they have failed more than they have succeeded, they have become aware of the moves required for success, and those are the moves they have to keep in the front of their mind. If, every time they get to a difficult move, they think back to their past mistakes, they will be held back. Instead, they need to be confident in their successes and their ability to complete the move. That means letting go of past failures and performing in the present, trusting that they will succeed.

Marriage is no different. If we intentionally take control of our thoughts, words and actions, we'll get into the "relationship zone." This is a wonderful place of presence, involvement and performance in which we can be natural and trust our relationship abilities. We know that we have what it takes to be a great spouse. We can be romantic and sexy because we can relax and be natural.

Every day we learn new things about our spouses that create "muscle memory," like how to approach them or how they communicate. Because we're constantly discovering new things about them, we need to be present, and aware of their responses to our actions. Developing that awareness may be hard won—we may do things wrong until we find a technique that generates a positive response—but a hard won success is no less sweet. We can view our mistakes as training, and move forward.

Summary

Faith is *now*. We live in the *present*. Our minds can swirl with stupid stuff about our partners every day, but we can change that by taking control of our thoughts, words and actions. We know that God gives us the strength to let go of past hurts so that we can make today the best day possible and anticipate a bright future. Having a partner with whom to share life makes each moment that much sweeter.

Road Map for Marriage

Questions for Reflection

1. Can you identify old baggage that is weighing down your marriage? What steps can you take to lighten the load?
2. Do you truly believe that God's mercies are new every morning, that He will forgive and give you the gift of a fresh start? Choose today to accept this gift.

Action Steps

1. Get into the "relationship zone". Honestly assess whether or not you are fully attentive and present when you interact with your spouse. Do you notice subtle reactions and cues that he or she uses to communicate, or are you often distracted by external factors like kids, TV and the phone? Write down some ways you can be more present with your spouse.
2. Is there an event or experience in your marriage that you need to "debrief" so that you can learn from it, put it behind you and move on? Set an appointment with your spouse to talk it through.

CHAPTER 5

FORKS IN THE ROAD
Healthy Decision Making and Communication

From mundane choices like what to have for dinner, to serious decisions like where to invest money, married couples engage in an endless stream of decision making. On one hand, we are thankful to have partners with whom we can make decisions—two heads are better than one, right?—but on the other hand, we all remember that life seemed more efficient when there was only one opinion to consider: our own.

In our travels we were constantly deciding where to go and how long to stay, but thanks to our lovely GPS, we didn't have to figure out how to get from place to place. We could simply relax and let her reassuring voice guide us through the turns until we arrived at our destination. There were some decisions, though, that our GPS couldn't help us with, like knowing how to handle unusually friendly camp mates at a Colorado camp ground. At that particular creek-side camp, the troublemaking neighbors were the black bears—"third generation garbage bears," as the local ranger described them. They made their rounds through the campground each night, pawing vehicles and knocking over anything between them and their food—coolers, mess kits, empty cans—which was followed by campers' various methods of scaring them away: shouting, setting off the car alarm, even firing a shot gun (a little extreme and definitely annoying at 4:00 a.m.).

One particular bear became quite well known when a camper caught site of her lounging by the creek. We returned to camp that evening to find ourselves playing a grown-up version of *Telephone*, the childhood game in which a message whispered at the beginning of the line is never the same at the end of it after being passed down a row of players. At the campground, we heard from some neighbors that the family from Texas next to them had heard from another camper further down the creek that a "1500-pound brown bear" had been spotted scarily close to the camp. A blurry, Sasquatch-like photo was being circulated as proof of the bear's size a nd proximity.

"We're leaving tonight!" exclaimed the Texans loudly to their fellow campers. "We've never seen anything like it! We're terrified! It's 1500 pounds! Brown! Might be a Grizzly! We're all in danger!"

It was difficult not to get caught up in the drama, but ultimately we were comfortable with our decision to stay where we were. The first step to reaching that conclusion was a confidence in our decision-making skills. We knew we communicated well and respected each other's opinions. We knew that we were usually able to think rationally and to view situations from multiple angles. Second, we didn't let emotions or fear dictate our decision. Finally, once the decision was made, we acted confidently, without regret.

Trust in our Teamwork

When we make mutual decisions with our spouses, we are demonstrating our trust in one another. Both trust and decision making improve with experience. During courtship, we practice making decisions like, "What should we do this weekend?" so that we are prepared to make more and more serious choices like "Where should we get married?" and "Who should raise the kids if something happens to us?"

When faced with our campground bear, we considered all the available facts in order to make the most educated decision possible. Gleaned from his many backcountry adventures, Josh's knowledge of bears allowed us to remain unemotional. We knew that the bear had been spotted in sites where food and cooking utensils had been left sitting out, so we could minimize our chances of being bothered by keeping our campsite clean and therefore unattractive. We researched facts about grizzly territory to reassure ourselves that we would not encounter one in that part of the country. Additional research on black bears' appearance and behavior ensured that we knew how to avoid provoking those that were our neighbors. Despite the dramatic warnings, we ultimately decided that we could stay put in our beautiful site—an example of refusing to let fear and emotion influence decision making.

When we work with each other to make decisions, we minimize the potential for finger pointing and blame if things go wrong. If Josh had just dismissed the problem by saying, "Don't worry. I know all about bears, we should just stay here," our experience would have been different. First, he would have missed an opportunity to check in with me—he would have ignored the possibility of my feeling nervous and needing reassurance that we were not being irresponsible. Second, if we had woken in the middle of the night to find a bear peering into the tent … well, we both would have been in trouble, but Josh sure would have shouldered most of the blame.

Practice and Preparation

Throughout our trip we spent as much time as possible checking the weather, searching for camping areas and researching trails—information that would help us make educated decisions. We empowered ourselves with the tools we needed to have the most enjoyable experience possible, because we wanted to do all we could to ensure a positive outcome. Because we had practiced this way of doing things, we could now trust that as a couple we made good decisions together. Even if things didn't turn out the way we intended after planning and preparing, making decisions together minimized our regrets. We didn't dwell on what we "coulda, shoulda, woulda" done if we had opted for something else. Instead, we could rest assured that we made the best possible decision with the information we had at the time. If we made a mistake, we learned from it and put it behind us.

Sometimes, decisions must be made on the spur of the moment. Quick decisions are usually the result of accumulated information stored in our subconscious minds. We may not be able to put a finger on why we "just know" something is right, but because we've read or heard it at some point before, we can view acting on instinct as the result of less intentional learning and training.

We saw an example of this at another camp site, where a neighbor was sleeping outside without a tent. He woke up in the middle of the night to see a bear standing a few feet away. He didn't have time to go online or find a book about how to avoid a bear attack. He simply had to react, so he summoned all his courage, and with the most ferocious voice he could muster, he roared "GRRRRR!" His tactic worked. The bear scuttled back into the forest and didn't bother him again. This was a time and place for a gut reaction to produce a quick decision!

Tuning in to the Still, Small Voice

Even when we give decision making our best efforts, we can't predict the future. We can only do so much with the information available to us, which is why Josh and I are happy to engage a higher power in guiding our decisions. We know that we can always rely on the still, small voice of the Holy Spirit to give us wisdom and discernment. We walk in faith by doing our part and trusting God to do His. God gives us the ability to research and evaluate. We rely on Him to guide us through that process, and then look for His blessing on our final decisions.

Sometimes, God's guidance may not align with our conclusions. Sometimes, we definitely feel in our spirits that we need to take an action that we hadn't planned or that doesn't seem logical under the circumstances. When that happens, we rest in the security that God knows the past, present and future, while we only see our miniscule place in time. We only know the natural, while He sees the supernatural. When He gives us wisdom beyond our understanding, we accept it. That wisdom is often revealed to us in subtle ways, so we want to be attentive.

It's easy to become confused between God's will for our lives and our own human selfishness. Psalms 37:4 gives us insight into that dilemma, promising that "if you delight yourself in the Lord, He will give you the desire of your heart." If we read that literally, we may interpret it as The Lord giving us anything we want. A more mature interpretation tells us that if we delight ourselves in the Lord, our desires will come into alignment with His desires for us. We'll find that the Lord first gives us the desire for something, and then He makes it reality. In that way, our wants align with His plans. Sometimes we feel that following Christ requires denying ourselves of everything we want, but if we open our hearts and allow Him to place those desires within us, we find peace and joy in having the things we want, because God has blessed them.

His Perfect Peace

Keeping this in mind when we are making decisions helps us avoid the spiritual battle between trying to figure out what we want and what God wants for us. That particular battle only creates stress and doubt. Say, for example, that a couple is car shopping and has narrowed their choices down to two cars. One would be comfortable, safe and affordable, and they feel good about buying it. However, in the back of their minds, they wonder if, as "good Christians," they should purchase the model costing $5,000 less, even though is doesn't seem to be the best option for their family. They don't feel at peace about denying themselves the car that they want. In such situations, it is important to remember that God never gives us stress and worry; He gives us perfect peace. So, the couple would be wise to make the purchase that gives them peace and give God thanks and glory for blessing their family with such great transportation.

Always remember that perfect peace always aligns with God's Word, because God doesn't contradict Himself. Desires from Him do not violate His commands. We can't fool ourselves into thinking that He gives perfect peace about having an extramarital affair, for example, which he clearly commands us not to do.

To receive His discernment, we have to delight ourselves in the Lord. When we set time aside for quiet introspection in His presence, we open ourselves to hearing the Word we've been seeking. While we tune into His desires, our selfish desires fade away. Sometimes, we have to die to self to experience the fullness of God's plan for us. In the same way, being willing to defer our own needs allows us to experience what is best for a marriage.

Obviously, not all decisions can be reached by utilizing research and checklists. Life demands tough decisions affecting our futures and our marriages, and tough decisions spark strong, emotional responses. In such instances we may need to use negotiation tactics, which are not always easy or comfortable. We have to practice them in order to figure out which techniques work best for our own unique relationships.

Whys not Whats

Negotiations look for "win-win" outcomes, so a good strategy is to use an interest-based approach. Prior to brainstorming or discussing solutions to a difficult decision, each party's interests must be out in the open, which means getting to the heart of *why* each partner wants to make a specific decision. Let's say that one spouse wants to move but the other one doesn't. It's easy to say "I don't want to move out of state, I want to stay here." That's a "what" statement, or a "position." All of us can easily identify *what* we want, but getting to the core of *why* we want it, or the "interest", can take some effort. To complicate matters, interests vary from the practical to the emotional. Interests can be things like, "I don't want move because we may lose money if we have to sell the house." Interests can be about how things are done, like, "We shouldn't move until the kids are older." Some interests are psychological issues, like "I have too many good friends here so I don't want to leave."

Once the various interests are initially out in the open, both partners can uncover sub-interests by asking questions like, "Why is that important to you?" or "How does that make you feel?" We keep asking those questions until we get to the root of the interest. Any time an answer is a position rather than an interest, we go beyond it and dig a little deeper.

For instance, a conversation may start with *"I don't want to move now because I'm afraid we will lose money on the house."* It would be easy to stop there and say "Ah ha, I understand now," but it would be wiser to keep asking why, to pursue a deeper discussion. For example:

"We worked hard to buy it together, and that's important to me because it represents something we did as a team."

"How do you feel about that?"

"If it becomes a bad investment, I will feel like we failed as a team".

"Why does that matter so much to you?"

"I think that our trust in each other might be compromised.

"How does that make you feel?"

"I'm afraid if we lose that trust, our marriage won't make it."

On the other hand, the other spouse's line of thinking might go something like this:

"I want to move because I think we need a change of scenery."

"Why is that important?"

"I don't want our life to become too routine."

"Why does that matter to you?"

"I don't want you to get bored with our marriage."

"How do you feel about that?"

"I'm afraid that if you get bored with me, you'll want to leave."

Cut to the Core

In this case, the couple doesn't need to judge how rational or realistic a core issue is, but they do need to get it out in the open and identify the perceived correlation between a move and a threat to their marriage. Rather than disagreeing about whether or not they should move, they can both agree that they don't want a move to threaten their marriage. From that point of agreement and from their core interests, they can develop a solution that addresses the position of each side.

When coming to a decision, it is important to remember that a consensus does not necessarily mean that the end result is both people's first choice. Consensus means that both parties are comfortable with the decision and will support it. They can support it because they have had the opportunity to contribute their opinions and express their feelings.

We must acknowledge a tendency to mask our deepest needs. It is more comfortable to talk in terms of the tangible, even when expressing the emotional. When a couple plans a vacation, for instance, one spouse may instantly express a desire to visit Costa Rica. The other may instantly prefer Cancun, so they argue and debate about which is the superior vacation spot. Instead of starting with a debate over the tangible, i.e. the location, they might be more productive by starting with questions that get to the more emotional side of the decision. "What do you want out of your vacation, and why do you think Costa Rica will give it to you?" The partner who is set on Costa Rica may confess to feeling bored or stifled at work, and as a result yearns for a sense of freedom and adventure. The other may be overwhelmed by helping family members deal with problems, and Cancun represents a place to relax and "just be." Suddenly the discussion becomes less about things. It's not a "you versus me" argument, resulting in a win-lose outcome. Now, rather than arguing about one place versus another, they can now explore a win-win discovery: both Cancun and Costa Rica have relaxing beaches *and* exiting activities.

Temperament Differences

Because decision making is such a major part of marriage, it can cause strife and tension if not done in a healthy way. Once we hone our skills, using them to make decisions becomes a blessing.

In many of my team building programs, I (Josh) encourage group members to become aware of their various social styles and to discuss how an awareness of the differences can help them work as a team. Social styles characterize dominant behavioral patterns. They don't represent deep beliefs or core values, but rather describe the ways we interact with people around us. The social style theory identifies four primary social styles. Read the descriptions of each, and see if you can identify yourself and your spouse.

1. **Drivers**: Give the impression that they know what they want, where they are going, and how to get there quickly.

Seek efficiency. Express thoughts about tasks rather than personal feelings.

2. **Expressives**: Appear communicative, warm, approachable and competitive. Involve other people with their feelings and thoughts. Enjoy being the center of attention. Often interrupt.

3. **Amiables**: Place a high priority on friendships, close relationships, and cooperative behavior. Appear to become involved in the feelings of others and relationships between people.

4. **Analyticals**: Live life according to facts, principles, logic and consistency. Often viewed as cold and detached but appear to be cooperative as long as they can have some freedom to organize their own efforts.

While it's impossible to sort our complex personalities completely, this quick assessment is a great discussion starter. When we understand our own social styles, we can understand how our interactions influence those around us. And when we understand our spouses' social styles, we can better help them into their comfort zones and maximize their contributions to decision making and problem solving. We can also interact with them in a much better way, and we can better recognize not only how to help them, but how to "help them help us."

Aminda knows that I am an "Amiable." I am a people pleaser and will agree to just about anything, including whatever she wants to do. It would easy for her to take advantage of that, as other people have done in the past. Instead, she makes sure that I share my opinions rather than just go along with what she wants. On the other hand, I know that Aminda is an "analytical." I recognize that she is flustered by decisions that can't be made using logic alone, and I understand that she has trouble letting go of her plans and routines.

Different personality types interact differently. When a "Driver" and an "Expressive" are working together, The Driver has to recognize the Expressive's need to talk through a situation (and yes, the Driver actually has to listen). Being in a partnership means showing temperance and empathy, and taking the other partner's ideas into consideration. Expressives can help Drivers by organizing their thoughts and opinions before sharing them, giving the driver a framework to more readily understand relevant information. If they learn to value each other's strengths—the Expressive's desire to talk through a situation and seek others' wisdom, and the Driver's ability to make timely and confident decisions—these two can have great success together.

So, rather than becoming flustered by how intense or passive or inconsiderate our spouses are when choosing a restaurant or redecorating the house, we can temper our reactions. We can remember that their reactions are simply part of who they are, and then practice harnessing their strengths.

Giving all to God

The *Maxwell Leadership Bible* contains an excellent study on keeping our priorities straight when making decisions. In his letter to the Philippians, Paul writes that

> what things were gain to me, these I have counted all things loss for the excellence of the knowledge of Christ Jesus my Lord, for whom I have suffered the loss of all things and count them as rubbish that I may gain Christ and be found in Him, not having my own righteousness, which is from the law, but that which is through faith in Christ, the righteousness which is from God by faith. (Phil. 3: 7-9)

Paul was focused on his priorities. Instead of basing his decisions on what was urgent or unfinished, he put first things first, let go of distracting hindrances, and then submitted fully to God's grace. Whenever in doubt, he let his decisions be guided by a single-minded pursuit of his calling. Verse 12 describes his passion for pursuing the prize of his call: ". . . I press on, that I may lay hold of that for which Christ Jesus has also laid hold of me."

The disciple James also advises us on solving problems effectively. "If any of you lacks wisdom, let him ask of God, who gives to all liberally and without reproach, and it will be given to him" (James 1:5).

King Solomon was a notable leader of Israel, helping the nation to prosper greatly. His great reign was jump started when, upon becoming King, he heard a question from the Lord which we all dream about, "Ask for whatever you want me to give you." It's pretty fun to dream about how we might respond to that question. Solomon however, was like that kid in class that was always kissing up to the teacher, asking God for "a discerning heart to govern your people and to distinguish between right and wrong" (1 Kings 3:9 NIV). The Lord was pretty impressed with this request. He not only made Solomon the wisest person alive, but also gave him bountiful riches and honor, setting a good example for generations to come.

Clearly, God wants us to seek wisdom and discernment. The more we exercise our God-given ability to distinguish between right and wrong, the more confidently we will make decisions, and the less we will be anxious and worried about worldly influences. We will truly be able to "walk by faith, not by sight" (2 Cor. 5:7).

Summary

Making decisions is a fact of life and a fact of marriage. When our lives are intertwined in marriage, it's crucial to work together, even when our differences make it hard to see eye to eye.

When we recognize and tap into our unique strengths, when we invest the time and effort required to work as a team in our decision making, we make better decisions with less conflict. We can use little day-to-day decisions as practice for making more complicated ones. Ultimately, we'll experience the benefits of investing in healthy communication and team work.

God gives us the wisdom and discernment to guide our choices, so we don't have to rely on our own strength or intelligence. While he doesn't promise us that things will always work out as we expected, He will help us recover and get back on track when they don't. Through His grace, we have freedom from regret and condemnation.

RoadMap for Marriage

Questions for Reflection
1. Do you allow regrets or past mistakes to influence your approach to decision making today? What is preventing you from forgiving yourself and putting that mistake behind you?
2. How do you respond when faced with a decision that you consider serious? Do you feel challenged? Energized? Overwhelmed? Scared? How do your feelings affect how you and your spouse make decisions together?

Action Steps
1. Discuss your unique communication and decision making styles. What are your strengths and weaknesses? Do you feel as though your spouse recognizes those strengths when you are making decisions?
2. Identify any areas of disagreement which may be grounded in "whats," then look for the "whys" at the root of the issue.

CHAPTER 6

BRAKE CHECK
Trusting your Life Partner

There were times during our trip when we went a few days between showers, yet even two or three days after our last shower, Josh managed to keep telling me that I looked beautiful. Given the unkempt state we were in, all I could say was, "I don't know how you can think that." It was hard to feel anything but disgusting, and when I felt disgusting, how could I possibly look beautiful? I was good at turning it into a joke: "You have to keep saying that out loud to remind yourself that I really am." With that attitude, I'm sure it didn't seem to Josh as though I believed he was telling the truth.

We've said in previous chapters that sometimes we have to be positive even when we don't feel like it, so if we're acting positive when we don't really want to, how are we supposed to trust what our spouses are *really* thinking and feeling? Because Josh is always so committed to being positive, how *was* I to know whether or not he was giving me an honest compliment?

For one thing, we know that feelings can be fickle. Life is full of things that we don't initially feel like doing. Like chores, or exercise. Once we break through those feelings and tackle the task at hand, however, we usually feel good about accomplishing it. So, even when we don't initially *feel* as though anything positive exists in a given moment, or when we don't *feel* as though we have anything nice to say about each other in a given situation, we can push through those feelings and find a positive, genuine thought. Thinking, acting and speaking positively doesn't mean being fake. It means rising above our emotions and establishing genuinely positive patterns that can be trusted.

Built Brick by Brick

The concept of trust, the "instinctive, unquestioning belief in and reliance upon something,"[1] is a complex but integral component of marriage. Does deciding to marry someone after a couple of years of courtship mean that we are declaring our unquestioning belief in and reliance upon that person? Newly married people often assume that their spouses must trust them wholeheartedly, no matter what, as soon as they tie the knot. This isn't an entirely fair assumption. Without actions to back them up, the words "you can trust me" are empty. Of course, we all want to be an amazing husband or wife who can be trusted completely, but our partners need to *experience* our trustworthiness in the same way that they need to experience our love.

We want our households to be safe places where we can express ourselves freely and without scorn, places where we are assured that any secrets will be kept in confidence. Trust is essential to fostering intimacy, and intimacy is at the core of good marriage. Trust, however, is not static. It continues to grow throughout a lifelong relationship. During courtship, men prove themselves trustworthy by doing such things as showing up on time for first dates, right after they trust women to give them the right address. As relationships progress, mutual trust continues to develop. The process can be compared to laying a tower, brick by brick. When a brick is added correctly, it will strengthen the tower. When one is added incorrectly, the tower is weakened. Trust is fragile, and we need to be aware of the ways we can build or damage it.

Demonstrating Dependability

How do we know that we are demonstrating trustworthiness? According to a 1998 study, five factors can be used to measure trustworthiness.[2] First, we care about others and demonstrate positive intentions. Second, we display honesty by telling the truth, accepting responsibility and avoiding manipulation. Third, we demonstrate openness by sharing power and decision making. Fourth, we are reliable and dependable. And finally, we are flexible, seeking conflict resolution.

1 Corinthians 4:2 (AMP) says, "Moreover, it is [essentially] required of stewards that a man should be found faithful [proving himself worthy of trust]." This verse explains that even though we have been entrusted with sharing the Gospel of Christ, we can't assume that we automatically deserve trust. God expects us to be faithful in both our words and our actions so that we can prove our trustworthiness to others.

From my (Josh) many years of experience working with corporate teams, I understand that trust is a key factor in strong, effective teams. Because trust is earned, team building activities are designed so that team members can practice building trust in one another. As a married couple, Aminda and I consider ourselves a team, and we also practice the principles of trust building.

In our careers, we expect that by proving ourselves in little things, like arriving to work on time and meeting deadlines, we'll eventually be entrusted with bigger projects. Marriage is similar. After the first few dates, we prove ourselves trustworthy by calling the next day, then by showing care and concern, keeping confidences, and so on. When our thoughtful actions become predictable, they foster trust.

A study of business teams found predictability to be an essential aspect of trust-building. Regular, predictable communication was more important than the quantity of communication for maintaining trust. Actions that separated high-trust teams from low-trust teams were simple: high levels of trust were correlated with reliability, demonstrated by such things as consistently and promptly acknowledging receipt of messages and informing team mates of absences.[3]

While it may not be reasonable to demand that our spouses trust us immediately and unconditionally, it is pretty easy to build trust through mundane daily activities, like telling them when we are going to be late from work, keeping date nights free and not sharing their secrets with others. If we prove ourselves trustworthy on a daily basis, they will be on our side when we ask them to trust us in matters of consequence. In marriage, both partners build a tower of trust, brick by brick. Both spouses contribute both by trusting their partners and by being trustworthy themselves.

Trust Roadblock: Low Self-esteem

By not taking Josh seriously when he told me I was beautiful, I demonstrated a lack of trust. By responding to his compliment in jest, I subtly implied that he was untrustworthy in what he said. He might have deserved my disbelief if he had suggested that I put on a little makeup or comb my hair, but he did nothing to deserve my skepticism, and I was just hindering his efforts to build his trust tower. Besides that, I sure didn't motivate him to keep up the compliments. A healthier reaction would have been to receive the compliment confidently. When your spouse demonstrates their high regard for you and you don't trust them, they'll stop making the effort. When they stop making the effort, it provides an actual reason to believe that they no longer think highly of you. So the trust tower crumbles, and real problems begin: you convince yourself they have lost interest or would rather be with someone else.

Low self-esteem can be a giant trust killer. When we think poorly of ourselves, we view our spouse's words and actions through our own filters of self-doubt. They can't give us the reassurance we need because our thirst for reassurance is never satiated: we are asking them for something that they can't give. A wife is only capable of giving her husband the love she has for him. She can't be responsible for giving him the love that he lacks for himself.

Love Yourself, Love Others

The Word tells us to "love your neighbor as yourself" (Gal. 5:14). This command rests on the assumption that we actually love ourselves to begin with. We have to be okay with loving ourselves and to be comfortable in our own skin, both of which are different from being prideful. To love ourselves is to love God's creation. It is to acknowledge that God loves us and that we are "fearfully and wonderfully made" (Ps. 139:14). It is not putting ourselves above others. When we are confident that we are amazing, we'll be able to treat people around us as though they are amazing, too, making them feel great.

While love from others can make us feel great, it has limitations. It was never meant to be a replacement for God's love or for the sense of self-worth that He provides. We are told that "the peace of God, which surpasses all understanding, will guard your hearts and minds through Christ Jesus" (Phil. 4:7). The world can be tough on self-esteem, saying "you're not good enough, you don't deserve this, you don't fit in here." When you are wounded by those fiery darts of negative thinking, your spouse can put a smile on your face, but only God's strong hands will prevent those fiery darts from permanently wounding your heart. Your spouse can give you warm fuzzies, but self-worth is intrinsic, stemming from a relationship with God. Relying on them to fill a self-esteem void is too much to ask, so release them from the responsibility of ensuring that you have a positive self-image.

Trust Block: Fear

At the root of low self-esteem is fear that we are not worthy or good enough. Fear is not a fun way to live. The Bible tells us not to fear—it is the opposite of faith. When we walk in fear, it's tough to have faith that our marriages are strong and lasting. We may fear our spouses' reactions if they discover something we are hiding, or we may fear they will leave us. We may fear that we'll just grow apart. In any case, fear always undermines our faith in marriage.

Divorce is so prevalent in our culture that fear of it can produce crazy behavior. Fear creates a cycle that's difficult to escape. When times are tough, you may convince yourself that your spouse will get fed up and leave. You both may become irritable and stressed, which makes it difficult to generate the positive behavior required to break out of the tough time. Fear must be rebuked, and the energy given to it, positively redirected.

Another common fear comes from hearing over and over again that children of divorce are more likely to end up divorced themselves. We can say "no" to that heritage. We can create new futures for ourselves. We can trust that God wants a new heritage for us and our marriages.

We previously shared a story about a bear that liked to steal food from one of our road trip campgrounds. Once the bear had been spotted, rumors and stories spread from campsite to campsite, and the bear became bigger and fiercer each time the story was passed on. In the same way, our imaginations can produce wild "what if" scenarios that create fear and worry. Rather than fretting and worrying, which allows our fears to become bigger and fiercer, we can give our worries to God. He is bigger than our problems, right? He gives us the right perspective on our challenges and keeps us from making mountains out of our molehills. Once we find relief from the snowballing effects of fear, we can return to his shelter of peace and trust.

Redirecting Fear

Aminda and I have found that in rock climbing, the most difficult obstacle to overcome is a lack of trust. New climbers have trouble trusting the equipment designed to protect them because they lack evidence that it will perform. They may not trust the person who is belaying them because they have never been belayed before. An element of fear is involved, in this case arising from a healthy need for self-protection. It isn't natural to ascend a cliff protected only by a thin nylon rope and what looks like a weatherproof belt. Trusting the unfamiliar requires faith in the unknown and the unseen.

Marriage presents a lot of unknowns. We feel pressured to do marriage right, but it's new territory. In addition, a healthy marriage may be unfamiliar to those who didn't have positive role models growing up, which simply means that they have some additional work to do. Most things in life have been unknown at some point—learning a sport, paying taxes, cooking Thanksgiving dinner. What did we do? We asked for help, watched YouTube videos, and practiced, practiced, practiced. We can apply the same effort to marriage. We can educate ourselves by reading books, talking to couples we respect, getting involved in small groups, attending seminars and classes. Any positive action takes our minds off fear and focuses our efforts on results.

Fear is the opposite of faith and is at the root of most negative emotions. In marriage, it can rear its ugly head in many ways. We may fear being controlled if we make the sacrifices expected from us. We may fear that we won't get what we expect or deserve from marriage, which often takes the form of jealousy when others seem undeserving of their circumstances.

Fear and worry sometimes seem nothing short of addicting. It's not always simple to turn either one of them off by telling ourselves, "Don't worry, be happy." Even so, awareness of habitual worry is the first step towards kicking it. Once we are aware of the habit, we can make an effort to actively challenge worrying thoughts, which requires discipline and self-awareness.

One of the problems with being preoccupied with worry is that worry tends to become self-fulfilling. It is also a huge energy siphon. When we are fearful, we spend time thinking about, talking about and researching the thing we fear. We can't afford to spend hours and hours fretting about whether or not to trust our spouses. We make things worse by talking endlessly with our friends about our worries. A positive response to worry is to redirect our nervous energy into action that will conquer what we fear. Moving past fear requires the same mental discipline as positive thinking—we recognize fearful thoughts and replace them with positive ones.

Envision and Overcome

When rock climbing, Aminda and I have experienced exactly how draining fear can be. When we encounter a difficult section, it's easy to doubt our ability and to fear that we are going to fall. Out of fear, we want to stop and stay put, so we don't fall. Time spent holding onto a rock wastes energy that could be better used to finish climbing the route. Only when the climber moves past that fear will they see the better holds above them that will get them through the difficult section.

Similarly, to transform fearful thinking we have to recognize fearful thoughts and conscientiously replace them with more positive ones, before we waste time held back in fear. People who believe that there is a will and a way to accomplish their goals will work harder to achieve them and are therefore more likely to attain them.

That's right: the most effective way to accomplish our goals is to believe that we can. So the first step towards attaining the peaceful, 50-year-long marriages we want is to believe we can have them. That confidence fuels the actions required to actually make it happen.

Fear is not only counterproductive, but also uncomfortable. While we hone our skills of replacing fear with productive thoughts and actions, we may experience discomfort. When that happens we can take some pointers from athletes, who use various mental techniques to maintain perspective on the discomfort that comes with intense physical exertion. In the sport of mountain biking, for instance, riding up hills is uncomfortable. It is a challenge to stay focused and motivated when the end of such intense exertion seems far away. A trick that can help is to pick an object up ahead, toss a mental bungee cord around it and let it figuratively pull you up the hill.

What if you applied that kind of thinking to every aspect of life? How would it be to look into your future and imagine your golden wedding anniversary, being more in love than ever, surrounded by friends and family? When in the midst of conflict, learn to throw a bungee cord around that vision and let it pull you forward. Envisioning success is far more productive than worrying about failure.

Trust Block: The Past

A healthy self-esteem paired with a no-fear attitude is a great set of tools for ensuring that our relationships are healthy and trusting—as long as we keep our pasts from infiltrating. We can't allow past relationships or other people's relationships to dictate the level of trust we have in our own spouses. If we do, we act out of fear. Our ability to trust our spouses must be based solely on who they are.

Before Josh and I married, I had been living alone for about five years. Living in a different state from my family had conditioned me to be very independent. Letting Josh come in and help out, as a man tends to do, took some adjusting on my part. Some things were easy to hand over, like killing bugs and mice, but to me, a girl who worked hard to stay strong and fit, his offers of help—whether it was a hand when crossing a rough section of trail or carrying in the groceries— came off as somewhat condescending. They weren't, of course. My reactions were based on my past. Once we were married, though, my independence could no longer be part of my identity. I had to let go and become part of a team. I couldn't let my past independence hinder me from receiving the love, care and protection that Josh was offering. I learned that when I opened myself to new experiences, and when I refused to let the past dictate my reactions, I freed myself to enjoy personal growth and new adventures.

Building Our Own Future

One sunny day in Crested Butte, Colorado, Aminda and I were enjoying a super sweet section of downhill mountain biking. Like Goldilocks, we had found a perfect trail—not too rough, not too steep, just a flowing descent with enough twists and turns to keep it interesting. Just the type of trail on which a cyclist can get so distracted by the beauty of his surroundings that he hits a root and loses control. Suddenly, he is launched over his handlebars, flying through the air like Superman before being not-so-gracefully deposited in the dirt. And that's exactly what happened to me.

After the crash, we rested for a couple of days while my bruises healed, and then we were back on the trail. I didn't blame my bike for failing me, and didn't blame the trail for letting me down. I didn't expect the next trail to cause a crash as the last trail had. I confidently rode the next trail with fresh eyes, expecting a brand new experience. If I had let the crash dictate my future experiences, I may never have ridden again.

In the same way, a disappointing past relationship doesn't mean that a new relationship will be disappointing, too. Even though I may have experienced or observed relationships characterized by hurt, betrayal and disappointment, if Aminda hasn't actually let me down, it's not fair to project other people's behaviors onto her. I have to let her build her own tower of trust, and I would impede that process if I were to expect her to behave like people who have caused disappointment in the past.

Instinctively, we want to protect ourselves from both physical and emotional pain. Just as we learn not to touch a burner on the stove, we learn to guard our hearts against situations that will cause emotional pain. If we let that become a habit, our hearts can become hard. That's why our best response is to surrender emotional pain to a higher power. We are promised that the peace of God will guard our hearts, so we need to relax and let Him fulfill His promises.

The scars from my crash didn't disappear completely. While faint, the physical marks are still there and likely always will be. In the same way, we can't expect our emotional scars to disappear completely. When our trust is betrayed, we are often left with tremendous emotional wounds and some scar tissue. But scar tissue is just scar tissue. We can still see it, it reminds us of a former wound, and it may even remain tender to the touch, but the intense pain that we suffered when it was inflicted is no longer there.

Accelerating Trust

Trust must be mutual. While we are making it easier for our spouses to trust us, we can also choose to trust them. When we feel that our partners have let us down, we would be wise to step back and consider their intentions before we consider our trust to be broken. How often do we overreact to a superficial comment or a grumpy glance? Given how well we know our spouses, one would think that we'd be able to see past surface behavior and immediately assume that they were distracted. Instead, we often get bogged down in our own issues and see them through our own lenses.

When I (Aminda) reacted to Josh's compliment, I jumped to conclusions. I immediately compared my appearance to how I may have looked at other times. My thoughts went to my oily hair and the pimple on my forehead. I probably thought about the other women I had seen that day and compared my appearance to theirs.

That was my "lens," but men and women think differently about compliments. A man doesn't compare his wife to every other beautiful person out there and dole out compliments based on how she measures up. He is simply saying, "I think you're a beautiful person, inside and out." Josh could see that I looked healthy, fit and relaxed after being outside for several days.

If I find it challenging to trust Josh's intentions, I try to talk to him about it. I can simply ask, "What did you mean by that?" and then be open to hearing his side of the story. Was the offense truly blatant disrespect or simply an honest mistake?

Create a Safe Place

In addition to trusting his or her intentions, it's also helpful to trust in your spouse's potential. You know your husband or wife better than anyone, and you can trust that they will mature and grow out of faults and weaknesses, that habits can change. You don't need to take the attitude that "he's never done that before, so he just can't do it." Instead, offering trust and positive reinforcement can be a huge contributor to positive change.

Sometimes you have to trust your spouse's way of doing things, even when their methods are different from yours. A staple in our road trip diet is peanut butter sandwiches. They are cheap, easy, relatively nonperishable, guaranteed to keep you feeling young, and they hold up well when squished into a backpack. When I (Aminda) am in charge of making the sandwiches, I spread even layers of peanut butter and jelly until they're flush with the edge of the crust. That way I can nibble little, equally tasty bites all the way around the sandwich. Josh's method is to plop a pile of peanut butter and an even bigger pile of jelly into the middle of the bread. That way he can eat the sandwich in three or four big swallows, and the outside is just a way to enjoy a couple of really amazing mouthfuls in the middle.

Neither way of making the sandwich is wrong. Neither of us is trying to convince the other that our own method of sandwich making is the only right one. We each trust that the other is a perfectly capable sandwich maker, just as we trust each other with the differences between the way we make the bed or wash the car. We work to separate "different" from "wrong." Is it worth risking an opportunity to demonstrate trust just to have something done my way? No. It's far better when I believe in Josh and encourage him to do things his own way.

Mitigate Risks

Another way to accelerate trust is to avoid situations that could destroy it. We don't want to be over-confident in our ability to resist temptation. Jesus instructed his disciples to "watch and pray so that you will not fall into temptation. The spirit is willing, but the flesh is weak" (Mark 14:38 NIV). When Jesus provided The Lord's Prayer as an example of how to pray, He included the petition "do not lead us into temptation but deliver us from the evil one" (Matt. 6:13).

Being tempted is not, in itself, sin. It is simply a situation that makes sin appear appealing and entices us to compromise our values. While God promises that we will not be tempted beyond what we are able, this promise rests on the assumption that our own carelessness or disobedience impedes his efforts.

Every weekend, thousands of people around the country go rock climbing. Most of those outings are uneventful, but occasionally a rock climbing accident results in injury or death. Josh and I choose to remain aware of the dangers, so every time we go rock climbing, we plan our outings as carefully as possible. While we could take risky shortcuts to save money or time, instead we take precautions to ensure our safety. We know how fast and how hard we are capable of climbing, so we honor our physical limits. We know the condition of the gear we use, and we stop using it before it wears out and no longer works as it should. We use maps and information to ensure that we understand the route we are climbing and to make sure that we stay on the right path. We avoid venturing out in dangerous weather. Can God perform a miracle and get us out of any situation we encounter? Of course. Does He also want us to use the brains that He gave us? For sure.

Every day, millions of happily married men and women interact with people of the opposite gender. Most of those interactions do not extend beyond a superficial connection. But some do. Some of those interactions eventually lead to affairs that damage or end marriages, so we want to mitigate risks in marriage much as we do in rock climbing. We avoid situations that make us more vulnerable to an affair, like hiding relationships from our spouses, spending time alone or having intimate conversations with the opposite gender, or consuming alcohol with them. Such precautions may seem silly or old-fashioned, but Matthew 26:41 warns us that our spirits are willing but our flesh is weak. We don't want our lack of judgment to damage our marriages any more than we want our lack of climbing judgment to lead to injury. Mitigating risk can be an important part of keeping the trust tower strong.

Summary

Trust is about being faithful and trustworthy in little things, because those little things are the bricks of the tower that will take our marriage to new heights. Trust is fundamental to a marriage relationship, yet it is scary because it requires us to be vulnerable. Mutual trust requires that we deal with some uncomfortable issues like self-esteem and past hurts.

We want to challenge ourselves to take the risk of actively building trust in our relationships. The reward will be worth the effort.

We will not fail to meet the challenge of building trust. Even when we struggle to trust our spouses, we can trust God unquestionably. Marriage is a cord of three strands, and even when our spouses disappoint or hurt us, the Third Strand keeps the relationships from unraveling. When our tower of trust crumbles, His guidance can help us rebuild.

RoadMap for Marriage

Questions for Reflection
1. Do you believe that your spouse must trust you 100 percent based solely on the fact that you are married? Or do you believe that trust grows and develops over time, based on your behavior?
2. Are you allowing yourself to be in potentially compromising situations? Do you need to remove yourself from tempting situations that could damage or destroy your marriage?
3. Are you confident enough to believe the compliments you receive from your spouse?

Action Steps
1. Talk to your spouse about your relationship fears. Discuss your feelings about divorce and how those feelings affect your reaction to conflict. How does fear impact both your vision and your feelings about a lifelong marriage?
2. Discuss any past hurts or mistakes which may be hindering your trust.

CHAPTER 7

SLUG BUG!

Cultivate a Healthy Sense of Humor

Before our trip, Josh's mom gave us a gag Christmas gift: a matching pair of dolls called Mr. and Mrs. Wonderful. When the dolls' hands are pinched, they spout off one of those clichés that every spouse supposedly wants to hear. For example, Mrs. Wonderful, in her warm and cheery voice, might say, "It's okay honey. I'll take out the trash today."

The suave Mr. Wonderful might respond, "Aawww, let's just cuddle tonight, Sweetie," or "I think I'll just pull over here and ask for directions."

These dolls traveled with us during our road trip, and they lightened the mood if it threatened to become too serious. "Did I say something annoying, Sweetie? Well, here, maybe Mrs. Wonderful will make you feel better."

A healthy sense of humor is not only a great tool for diffusing tension, but it also helps us maintain that flow of positive thinking. God wants us to laugh. Job 8:21 tells us that "He will yet fill your mouth with laughing, and your lips with rejoicing." Joy is a fruit of the spirit, given to us as a gift. Hundreds of verses in the Bible promise God's joy, which we express in singing, dancing, smiling, shouting and laughing. Laughter is a way of expressing our joy in the Lord.

Psalms 126: 2-3 reveals that laughter can also be a way to express confidence in God's goodness: "Then our mouth was filled with laughter, and our tongue with singing... the Lord has done great things for us, and we are glad."

Healthy Humor

Research has confirmed a connection between laughter and both physical and emotional health. The International Society for Humor Studies exists to research and promote the benefits of humor. What have they and other researchers found? Plenty. Laughter has been shown to:

- Relax the body, relieving muscle tension and physical stress.
- Boost the immune system by decreasing stress hormones and increasing immune cells and infection-fighting antibodies.
- Make us feel good by triggering the release of endorphins, the body's natural feel-good chemicals, which can even temporarily relieve pain.
- Protect the heart by improving the function of blood vessels and increasing blood flow, which can help protect against cardiovascular problems including heart attacks.
- Stimulate organs by enhancing the intake of oxygen-rich air, which stimulates the heart, lungs and muscles.[1]

Another study showed that laughing improves digestion, and that laughing 100 or more times throughout the day may have similar health benefits to 10 minutes of aerobic exercise.[2] Studies have even shown a correlation between a healthy sense of humor and a healthy sex life.[3]

On the flip side, stress and depression can contribute to a myriad of ailments including stomach conditions, skin reactions, heart disease and sleep problems. Chronic anxiety and tension have been found to double the risk of disease, and depression has been shown to hinder recovery from illness and disease. It's no wonder that Proverbs 17:22 tells us, "A cheerful heart is good medicine" (NIV).

Good moods not only have physical benefits, but emotional ones as well. A positive mindset improves the flexibility and complexity of our thinking, making it easier to find solutions to both intellectual and interpersonal problems, and enhancing our ability to foresee the consequences of a given decision. Laughter has many relationship benefits, too. In fact, it's been theorized that the health benefits attributed to laughter may be less about the physical act of laughing and more about the social support that laughter encourages. Think about it. How often do we tell a joke only for ourselves? How much more likely are we to enjoy a good belly laugh with others than when alone?

Chuckling our Way to a Closer Connection

Most of the happily married couples we know have developed a shared sense of humor. They know how to make each other laugh—how to turn the other's frown upside down. Those special inside jokes that only the two of them understand, those knowing sideways grins from across the room—that sort of camaraderie is one of the beautiful aspects of marriage. Humor can actually be a way of indicating alignment or satisfaction between partners.

Humor is an important indicator of relationship interest. A sense of humor indicates a high level of emotional and social intelligence, i.e. the ability to say the right thing at the right time and to the right people. A humorous exchange indicates mutual appreciation, while a failed attempt can subtly signal rejection—not only of the joke but of the person.

Both men and women like a partner with a sense of humor. The bond created by humor starts during courtship. In early relationship stages, women are more likely to be attracted to men they find funny, while men are attracted to women who laugh at their jokes. So during courtship, men are generally focused on being the funny guy. Once courtship is over, though, gender differences become less defined. Women are just as likely to be funny as men, and men are just as likely to appreciate humor in women.

Couples often develop their own unique, shared humor. Thankfully, they don't have to be entertainers or comedians to be funny. Any couple can share a secret humor language, whether exchanged in words, expressions, signals or touch. Words aren't even necessary—it's easy to send a silly card or funny email to share a laugh.

Honing our Humor

One way Aminda and I lighten the mood is by turning conversations into funny songs. Since neither of us are accomplished singers, we're probably the only ones who find these songs entertaining. We integrate personal stories, obscure movie quotes and other lyrics that would be downright puzzling to outsiders. We like to belt them out when we are high on a rock face, hundreds of feet above the ground, where it seems as though we're the only people on earth within range of our voices (since no one else in the world should have to hear our singing).

As relaxed as we are together, we don't always rely on humor to come naturally. Each of us pays attention to what brings the other joy and laughter, just as we each pay attention to what makes the other feel loved, scared or engaged. I know Aminda won't laugh at the same old jokes year after year—I've got to keep it fresh. Aminda definitely makes me chuckle with a silly dance move or, well, a fart (I'm a guy). But she's also observed that what really makes me laugh out loud are movie quotes, so she's honed her skills at delivering movie lines. (Turns out she's on to something—surveys have actually found that the style of humor us men appreciate most from women is very similar to their own: sarcastic and juvenile.)[4]

Whether silly or sarcastic, humor can turn blah days into good days, and good days into great days. It keeps us feeling young even as we age, and it helps us weather life's storms and struggles. Integrating humor into relationship challenges can help us:

- Clear our minds, and see our troubles from a different, less threatening, perspective
- Release defensiveness, criticisms, and doubts
- Open up, releasing fear of holding back
- Express our true emotions

The Not-So-Serious Side of Stress

Earlier we mentioned that low self-esteem can hinder trust and closeness in relationships, including the bond developed through humor. Without a healthy self-image, it's hard to relax enough to let go and be funny. Having a well-developed funny bone comes with a risk of embarrassment—laughing out loud at inappropriate moments, appearing politically incorrect, enduring long awkward pauses when a joke is misunderstood. "Don't take yourself so seriously" is the cardinal rule of humor.

When I (Aminda) pulled out Mrs. Wonderful, Josh could easily have been defensive or accused me of mocking him. Instead, he chose to react with love and joy—he knows we have to be able to laugh at ourselves. It's healthy to find humor in our mistakes, weaknesses and shortcomings. This should be particularly easy to practice around our spouses. They know our weaknesses better than anyone, and they love us despite all. Together, husbands and wives can find humor in the past, reflecting on and laughing at how immature they were in the early days, and giving thanks for how they've grown together.

A couple we admired for their particularly fun-loving relationship is a great example of how humor can reduce stress. The husband had a glass eye and didn't hesitate to make jokes about it. Fred would sometimes casually drop the eye in his wife's water glass just to enjoy her reaction. The two of them made the most of intense Phoenix summers by spending nights playing in the pool, and then jumping straight from the pool into their bed on the outside sleeping porch. It was this playful attitude that kept them strong during his eventual battle with terminal cancer.

We may not welcome jokes when stressed, but it can help to be receptive. Jokes during tough times require careful timing, because making light of a serious situation at the wrong time can backfire and exacerbate already intense emotions. However, when our trusted partners makes light of an issue that is upsetting us, it's probably because they can see we are overacting. By helping us settle down a little, they're actually doing us a favor—we'll be able to deal with the circumstances more quickly when our moods are lightened a bit.

In any stressful situation or discussion, we want to use humor carefully. We want to respond slowly, choose our words carefully and evaluate how those words will be interpreted. It's a balance that can take some practice to master, but one that's worth the results. We have two friends who have learned how to respond to frustrating situations. When one of them gets grouchy or discouraged, the other will say, "Sounds like someone needs the tickle monster." (When someone is at a loss for words, tickling is an easy way to get a good, healthy laugh.)

Television host and surgeon Dr. Oz explains that it's not so much the stressor that causes problems as it is our reaction to it. We can't get rid ourselves of our jobs and circumstances. We can, however, deal with them in a healthy way, and laughing is one of the healthy ways to relax and reduce stress. A pregnant woman, for example, who worries over an alcoholic beverage or cigarette before learning she was pregnant, can actually cause more harm to the baby with that stress than from the substances she had consumed.[5]

Mourning into Laughing

When we've seen all the health benefits of laughter, it's easy to believe that we can stay fully energetic right up until the end. The Bible regularly guards us against fear and worry. Job 5:22-26, which tells of the protection God offers when we allow him to guide our ways, says "You will laugh at destruction and famine... you will know that your tent is secure; you will take stock of your property and find nothing missing... you will come to the grave in full vigor" (NIV).

This is an inspiring passage. It's easy to give the enemy more credit than is due. But the enemy doesn't have any power in our lives—we have been redeemed. When the enemy uses his wiles to make us fearful, we can laugh at his weak attempt. When the storms come, our tent is secure. When the economy is down, when your home value is falling and prices are rising, you know it is just a weak attempt to get you to covet another's fortune or to lose faith in God's provision. We don't have to be distracted by those earthly worries. We are not of this world. Our faith is in God, in Whom our home is secure, who is the One who tells us "I will turn their mourning into gladness; I will give them comfort and joy instead of sorrow" (Jer. 31:13 NIV).

Research has shown memory to be state-specific, which means that we're more likely to reflect on positive events while we are in a good mood than we are in a poor mood. As our summer road trip drew to an end, Josh and I sat around the campfire at night and reminisced. We were done with planning and problem solving, and in that relaxed, contented state, we didn't reflect on bad weather or unwelcome rodents. Our minds only conjured up only the amazing summits, spectacular scenery and memorable accomplishments. Our happy reminiscing was a therapeutic way to deal with the end of an amazing summer.

The ability to make light of challenging events is considered a natural self-defense mechanism. When we turn to humor in the face of adversity, it buffers us and prepares us to endure what is to come. When we actively focus on laughing off problems, we spend less mental energy worrying about what's to come. When trouble passes, joy and laughter signal recovery, and we're more likely to know that everything is going to be all right.

Keeping Humor Healthy

More often than not, humor is healthy and helps us deescalate conflict. However, there are humor habits that we need to avoid, like laughing at someone else's expense. Even though we learned this rule in elementary school, it can be hard to follow, even as adults! As we've seen, humor carries power and influence. It can improve circumstances for the better, but it can also be selfishly misused to manipulate or embarrass others.

Laughter has two sides. It expresses joy and mirth, but also ridicule. We want to make sure that we don't cross the line and hurt anyone. Because it's okay to laugh at someone purposefully dressed in a funny costume, for example, it's hard not to laugh at someone who is unintentionally dressed oddly. This type of laughter is mockery and scorn, and it doesn't feel good on the receiving end. We see this type of laughter in the Biblical books of Job and the Psalms, when Job and David are mocked and insulted by their enemies. While our own intentions may be innocent, we can't afford to engage in mockery and insult. Neither is characteristic of the Christian heart that we want to foster.

In his book, *The Relationship Cure*, John Gottman emphasizes the importance of checking our attitudes and not allowing humor in our relationships to drift into insults, name calling, mockery or sarcasm.[6] When this type of hostile humor is directed at a spouse, it is a sign that the health of the marriage is in serious decline from which recovery is difficult.

We want to watch for subtle signs that our humor is taking a turn towards antagonism. A frequent "just kidding" approach can feel more like insults than lighthearted teasing, and it signals that the line between healthy and unhealthy humor has been crossed. A veiled joke is really a way to avoid taking responsibility for an insult.

There are right times and wrong times to joke around. Making a joke to change the subject when our partners brings up something that we don't want to talk about, like finances or chores, eventually leads to them laughing less and becoming frustrated that they can't talk to us about anything important. Yes, humor can help calm us down or put things in perspective, but we must take care not to placate our spouses with it to avoid addressing an issue or to ignore their needs. Before we accuse a partner of being unable to take our jokes, we need to examine our motives. Were the jokes positive, helpful and healthy, or were we sliding into unhealthy uses of humor? Always direct the power of humor into building up, not tearing down.

Summary

A fisherman married a landlubber. On their wedding day, her vows included the line: "I solemnly vow never to interfere with my husband's annual chase for a winner in the fishing derby." This is the kind of healthy humor that will keep marriage relationships close—when we choose to make light of a subject which could be a source of contention.

If we can't muster anything nice to say, there's one action to try. Smile. Sure, we can always fake a smile, but smiling can trick the body into helping us change our moods. It's almost impossible to hold a fake smile without it turning into a real one. If nothing else, we feel so goofy about a big, fake grin that we can't help but chuckle at ourselves.

Smiling may make you appear even more attractive to your spouse. Smiles draw others to us because they signal that we have something—a positive feeling—that they want. Smiling is contagious, so by changing your own outlook, you can easily improve your spouse's as well. Smiling and laughing relieves stress and releases endorphins, natural feel-good chemicals that give you a mini emotional high. Since studies have shown a correlation between big, happy grins and a longer life-span, it could be said that the couple who smiles together, stays together.

Road Map for Marriage

Questions for Reflection

1. What's your favorite source of humor—movies, cartoons, your favorite uncle? How can you find more humor in your life? Hang out with kids or pets?
2. What healthy ways do you use to lighten a heavy mood or diffuse a tense situation?
3. Can you identify any ways that you use humor to avoid responsibility?

Action Steps

1. Pay attention to the things that bring your spouse the most laughter and joy. Make a list of ways you can make them happen more often.

CHAPTER 8

THERE'S ONLY
ONE DRIVER'S SEAT
Designating Roles

When Aminda and I first started camping together, I was the more experienced camper, so we used my gear, my truck and my organizational system. We'd arrive at our destination, and I'd hustle about, unload bins, set up the tent, fire up the stove and start dinner. Aminda helped a little by carrying boxes or chopping vegetables, but she mostly felt awkward trying to fit into my routine. All that has changed now, because over time we have developed our own rhythm. Now we both hop out and know exactly what each of us needs to do. We quietly go about our work, then relax and chat as we enjoy our meal under the stars.

Life runs more smoothly with structure and organization. Developing a rhythm can eliminate a great deal of strife. When members of a team share responsibilities, they reduce both the burden of delegation and the amount of work that a single individual must carry.

When two people both feel in control of their own space, it's easier for them to agree about how to share work. Taking responsibility for our own tasks gives us purpose and order, which enables us to focus more on what we *are* doing than on what our partners are not doing. Orderly cooperation minimizes nagging and frustration.

The two of us fell into our camping routine because we have different strengths and weaknesses. For example, experience has given me some pretty remarkable organizational and packing skills, so when we break down camp, I ensure that the vehicle is ready to hit the road. We also place different degrees of importance on tasks. Aminda is concerned that we're fed and hydrated, so she takes charge of packing lunch and filling our water bottles.

We also have different strengths in climbing, which benefits us when we are sharing responsibility for leading a route. We each select pitches that give us the best chances of success, which in turn makes them more enjoyable. Everyone likes to do what they do best, because it feels good to excel at something, to shine.

In his letter to the Roman church, the apostle Paul explains that "we have many members in one body, but all the members do not have the same function ... Having then gifts differing according to the grace that is given to us, let us use them ... " (Rom.12:4-6). God has blessed all of us with unique gifts and talents. Because we all have different strengths, we can accomplish more together than we can alone. By contributing our gifts to a team—whether the team be the church or a marriage—we serve those around us.

Nurturing a Spirit of Service

As we were planning our wedding, Josh and I discussed our expectations for marriage. At some point during one of those conversations, he revealed that one of his plans to ensure a happy marriage was always to "out-serve" me. Now, having a slight competitive streak, I responded, "Oh yeah? I might just have to make sure that you can't out serve me." I took his statement as a challenge—the most positive of challenges, of course. Years later, we're still making an effort to out-serve each other. It's amazing how much difference it has made. Instead of grumbling when Josh doesn't take out the trash, I know I can serve him by doing it without nagging. (Of course, he's so committed to service that he rarely neglects the trash.) This challenge might backfire if we were keeping score, so we play it as though each of us always needs to catch up to the other. Even though we may not feel like doing something, we've learned that we just have to push ourselves, to challenge ourselves and push past our feelings. We have decided that we want to be bigger persons by committing to our word and upholding our responsibilities. This requires that we consciously develop the intent of our hearts by purposefully serving and blessing others.

We stay motivated to serve each other because we assume that we're both held to the same standards—we trust that we're both trying to give our best to our marriage. A competition of service is healthier than a competition of self-sacrifice. There is no reason to fall into the martyrdom trap, where we develop the mindset that we must deny our own needs for the sake of the relationship. We can't refuse assistance from others and then take on the mindset that we are the only one in the marriage who is contributing and sacrificing.

We saw an example of this play out at a California campground:

"Ahhhhaaaaaa!!!! My EYES!!! Ohhhhh!!!! My EYES!!! OOOwwww!!! Noooo!!!" The loud wails exuded pain and agony. We stood by helplessly and watched the social, upbeat young man we had met just a few minutes ago. The cloud of smoke from the campfire he was starting was stinging his eyes.

"Hey, do you need some help?" ventured one of his friends.

"No, Man, I'm okay," the fire-starter calmly replied before returning to poking and prodding his creation, which would set off another wail. "My EYES!!! Ahhhhaaaaaa!!!! Noooo!!! My EYES!!! OOOwwwweeeeeeee!!!"

This confusing exchange repeated itself a couple more times. Friends would offer help, Fire-starter would insist that he needed nothing, then continue with agonizing wails that would have had us calling for help had we not been right there to see that his life was not endangered.

We can generate attention by resisting help, but we probably won't succeed in getting our needs met, in or outside of marriage. If we feel that an imbalance exists in our marriage, we may have to be more direct or specific in telling our spouses what we need. Pretending that we don't have any needs is counterproductive. Part of being in a relationship is letting our spouses serve us, and it should make us feel good to serve each other.

Gottman describes a characteristic of a dysfunctional relationship: one partner will respond to a request by saying, "You don't get your needs met in this relationship? Well, too bad, but I don't get my needs met, either." Instead, we need to be bigger than that by responding, "You don't get your needs met? That's wrong! Both of us should be satisfied in this relationship, so let's figure out how to make that happen."[1]

If a woman needs her husband to help out around the house more, if he just can't seem to do things well enough to meet her standards, she can try setting him up for success. She can identify his strengths and the tasks he does best, and then give him the tools he needs to get the job done. If, for example, she'd like to delegate the grocery shopping, she could make sure that he has a detailed list to follow (maybe create a photo list on his smart phone). If he loves grilling, she might give him some recipes that she'd like to try which would provide variety and balanced nutrition for their family. A wife can always help her husband to be helpful, especially if she remembers that his way of doing things may be different. And different is just different—it doesn't mean his way of contributing is sub-par. When each individual in the relationship has purpose and is set up to contribute his or her own unique talents successfully, the needs of both are more likely to be met.

Opposites or Complements?

When Josh and I are in touristy areas like national parks, other people reinforce our unique strengths. Josh has this friendly, open face that looks like he's just waiting to lend a hand. When people need a picture taken, he's their guy. He's the one who will stand awkwardly in the middle of a crowded sidewalk, clutching a stranger's camera, and wait for a family of 10 to position themselves perfectly in front of the west coast's oldest living barrel cactus.

I, on the other hand, am a little more type A, so I'm usually moving fast with a purpose. This air of "I know exactly where I've been, where I am and where I'm going" makes me the person who must have directions to everything from the nearest Dollar Store to California's finest petting zoo. Whether I am around the block from my house or in downtown Beijing, I am frequently approached for assistance. So, when Josh and I are together, the lost tourist who would like to capture the moment with a picture is in luck!

We have different temperaments, but we obviously have a lot in common, too, like our love of the outdoors and adventures. Would we describe our relationship as a case of "opposites attract," or "birds of a feather"? That old adage, "opposites attract," actually has some negative connotations. "Opposite" infers that two things are contrary, incompatible or irreconcilable. When communication and problem solving become difficult for opposites, it might be easier for them to come up with scapegoats: "Well, we're just opposites; it's no surprise that we have problems," or "We'll never get past our differences—might as well just throw in the towel." Such attitudes couldn't be further from the truth. While it may be challenging for "opposites" to cooperate, some degree of contrast between spouses is a beneficial to marriage.

Two people who think and do things differently can "complement" each other, which means that they complete one another or make each other perfect. Rather than viewing your spouse's personality as opposite from your own, it's wiser to recognize the core values and faith that are shared. In that way, you see the ways in which your spouse's unique perspectives and ideas provide a more holistic view. If you look, you can see how their strengths minimize your weaknesses and complete you as a team.

His and Her Roles

Differences between men and women are a result of many factors, including their intrinsic complementary design. Men instinctively operate from a need to be the provider and protector, while women are caretakers and nurturers. When we're, say, identifying the ideal campsite, Josh looks at factors that might influence safety. What are the neighbors like? Are there any large trees that could fall on our heads? On the other hand, I as the caretaker place priority on having a water source that can supply our cooking and cleaning needs.

We're not trying to limit women to the kitchen and men to the garage. This isn't about having interests, talents or personality characteristics that fall into gender stereotypes. We are blessed to live in a time and in a country where both men and women have the freedom to provide for their families and fulfill their roles in whatever way they choose. These roles are less about "how and who" than they are about the goals of loving, providing for and supporting each other in our own unique ways.

We can also be mindful of letting our spouses fulfill their God-given roles. Some of us may need to step out of the way and stop trying to do everything on our own. Men and women are wired differently and are biologically different. Those differences are designed for partnership. Men and women are designed to play different, complementary roles in the household and in life.

The Pew Research Center has found that since the late 90's, the number of women aged 18 to 34 who say that a successful marriage is among the most important things in their lives has risen, while the percentage of men agreeing with the same statement has dropped. Why is this? One theory[2] is that women have increasingly been encouraged to play both roles in the household. When they do this, they push men off their pedestals and stop seeing their value. Much of men's satisfaction and self-esteem comes from knowing that they are fulfilling their purpose. So when women try to fulfill both male and female roles, men are robbed of their purpose, making marriage less appealing.

Men want to love and care for women, not to compete with them. They want to provide for and protect their families—it's in their DNA. Modern women can choose to let them, without diminishing female ability or independence.[3] A woman can graciously let a gentleman open a door for her, even though she's been opening her own doors all day. Encouraging men to love and care for women doesn't mean that husbands and wives can't contribute to a relationship equally, nor does it mean that men can't take care of the kids. But when push comes to shove, men have to step up and ensure that the family is provided for. No matter how capable a woman is, it's not a man's role to sit by idly while his wife works multiple jobs to provide for the family.

The woman described in Proverbs 31 is held up as a timeless example of a strong, accomplished, yet feminine woman; she is a land and business owner in addition to being a wife and mother.

> She is clothed with strength and dignity; she can laugh at the days to come. She speaks with wisdom, and faithful instruction is on her tongue. She watches over the affairs of her household

and does not eat the bread of idleness. Her children arise and call her blessed; her husband also, and he praises her.... Honor her for all that her hands have done. (Prov. 31: 25-31 NIV)

Does this sound like a woman who has been held back or put in her place by the men in her life? Not at all. She sounds like a woman who holds her own and has been blessed for embracing and maximizing her God-given ability.

A line from *My Big, Fat, Greek Wedding* is, "The man is the head of the house, but the woman is the neck, and she can turn the head any way she wants." That's a pretty big responsibility! If the neck moves too roughly or hastily, it risks damaging both itself and the head. Instead, women want to exercise controlled, gentle movement. A gentle spirit carries tremendous power. Within a spirit of willing submission is influence.

Ephesians 5:23 states that "the husband is the head of the wife." If we take a closer look at the man's role as head of household, we see that "head" does not mean ruler, but rather means "first," like the one who rides into battle before the troops. The man's responsibility is to protect the home, to take authority, to fast and pray and do whatever it takes to keep his family whole. God doesn't want us to control others; He wants us to surrender our lives to Him, to let Him assume control. A real man stands for justice, liberty and goodness, and he is willing to fight for it all. That is the nature of the masculine heart.

Paul's teachings on marriage, which instruct women to submit and be silent, are also controversial because they are easy to misinterpret when taken at face value. Taking a closer look at the term "submit," we see that Paul's original word means something more along the lines of "be supportive of," or "allegiant to," which are the exact attitudes that a woman should want to assume as a wife. Being in a marriage, which is a team, is all about spouses supporting each other.

Ephesians 5:22 instructs women to submit to their husbands, and then instructs men to "love your wives just as Christ loved the church and *gave himself up for her.*..." Think about the gravity of that command. Christ gave his life, the ultimate sacrifice, for the church. If our husbands are taking their roles seriously—loving us with that type of sacrificial love and putting our needs ahead of their own—we should have no problem trusting them to fulfill the role of head of household that God designed them to be.

Men are designed to be competitive and to conquer, but women want to be rescued rather than conquered. Jesus came to this earth to rescue His bride, not to conquer her. He conquered the enemy. Jesus came to rescue His bride no matter what it took, and He laid down His life. Men need to step up confidently and take on the responsibilities expected of them. As heads of their households, men cannot abuse their roles by letting selfish pride get in the way. Jesus deserved all the respect and riches of this world, yet He humbled himself and sacrificed it all for His bride. The Bible warns men against being harsh with their wives and directs them to be gentle, kind and compassionate. If the Bible instructs men in this way, we can be sure that obeying that direction is masculine.

There is no reason either to ignore or to fear gender roles. We need not resist who we are or succumb to society's pressures to become someone else. Men and women are genetically different, and it's okay to recognize and utilize the differences for the benefit of our relationships. Respecting gender differences is more about nurturing an attitude of service than about fulfilling specific tasks. God's gender roles guide us in sharing overall responsibility for the well-being of our household; they don't define who cooks and who takes out the trash.

Summary

Because marriage is a beautiful joining of two unique individuals, spouses' complementary differences enable them to develop a rhythm—a relaxed, productive state in which they accomplish more together than they do alone. They are stronger as a team than as individuals.

Even with good attitudes, we will occasionally be frustrated by each other's differences. When that happens, it's best to acknowledge each other's feelings, and then deal with them by refocusing on how important those differences are on a winning team. We're better off if we relax, rejoice in each other's differences, learn from one another's strengths and encourage each other to be awesome.

Everyone feels good when contributing and serving, so when we seek opportunities to encourage our partners' strengths and gifts, we encourage them to succeed, to shine and to keep giving their best to the relationship. When we are committed to cultivating this attitude of service, we minimize discord over unmet responsibilities and we create more opportunities for praise and appreciation.

RoadMap for Marriage

Questions for Reflection

1. In what ways does your marriage relationship imitate that of Christ and his church?
2. What do you feel is your greatest contribution to your spouse and/or family? Do you feel that your partner encourages you in this role?
3. In what ways do you encourage your partner's strengths?
4. What were you originally taught to believe about Paul's writings in Ephesians? Do you believe it is offensive to women?

Action Steps

1. Brainstorm analogies that you can use to relate your marriage to a team. Is one of you a good offensive player and one of you good at defense? Are you a homerun batter and a strikeout pitcher?

CHAPTER 9

ARE WE THERE YET?

Finding Healthy Alone Time

They say that absence makes the heart grow fonder. If that's so, what happens when a couple spends 90 days together with no absence from each other? I (Aminda) didn't know what to expect, but my reaction to our first day apart was a surprise. We had arrived back in northern Arizona one day before Josh was scheduled to guide a rafting trip on the Colorado River. He met the group in Flagstaff, and while he was gone, I camped out there until we could return to our home in Phoenix. The first morning that I woke up without Josh, I was struck with such a profound sense of loneliness that I cried.

It was a highly unexpected reaction—we had, after all, regularly traveled separately throughout our marriage—but feeling so lonely made me realize what a joy it had been to have my best friend so close for the last three months.

Although we assumed, going into the trip, that we'd each need some time alone along the way, we discovered that we didn't. We did almost everything together all the time, which meant we had to be okay with periods of quiet. During long drives or in our tent after dinner, for example, I spent hours reading or writing, letting Josh have his thoughts to himself.

Ultimately, the amount of time we physically spent together or apart wasn't as important as creating space for one another just to chill—times when we didn't have any issues to talk about, when we didn't have to entertain, please or support each other. It's the same in daily married life: couples who have a difficult time just "being" when they are together might need to plan more physical time apart, where they have enough time and space to chill.

Marriage presents us with occasions when we are upset—when we need to take a break, count to ten and calm down before we continue a charged discussion. We occasionally need to walk away from a situation to decompress, sort out negative thinking, and regain control over our thoughts. We also need time apart for constructive reasons. Solo time should be positive and refreshing. It shouldn't be an excuse for "I just don't want to hang out with you anymore," and it's definitely not time to build up reserves for the next argument.

A couple who had been married more than thirty years had almost stopped communicating because of financial stress caused by the husband being out of work. Eventually he accepted a contract position 200 miles away and came home only on weekends. Ultimately, that move gave them the space they needed to reevaluate and appreciate their marriage. It took a break from their all-consuming fear and worry to bring the rest of their marriage—all that was good and Godly—into focus.

Regain Perspective

All rock climbers encounter difficult sections of a route, and when they do, they are sometimes challenged by "tunnel vision" produced by fear. Suddenly, they can see nothing but the small holds directly in front of them, and they freeze in place. They have trouble adjusting their positions and looking for holds that can help them unlock the move and advance upward.

We don't want tunnel vision in our marriages. We don't want to get so wrapped up in our own irritations that we lose perspective. When minor frustrations consume us and we can't see beyond our own small worlds of hurt, we need to rest and regain control, just like challenged climbers. Constructive solo time is healthy rest, and it can add fuel to our relationship reserves.

Sometimes a little space is all that is needed to regain perspective. You don't have to be hundreds of miles apart for months at a time; you might just need enough time without your spouse to notice the void left by their absence—the special contributions they make to the marriage which aren't being filled—to realize how much you depend on them. And for those couples who do end up spending extensive time apart? Well, they can look forward to an exciting reunion.

Alone but not Lonely

It's possible to feel lonely in both a crowd or in a relationship, which means that loneliness has little to do with how many people are near. Being contented when we are physically alone, starts with being comfortable in our own skin, secure and at ease with who we are. While we can't blame our spouses' absence for chronic loneliness, it's true that a dependable, intimate marriage is beneficial to our personal well-being. Relationships protect us from a sense of isolation and can mitigate the health risks created by stress, anger and depression.

Close, loving relationships are associated with good health, which makes missing your spouse's company normal. However, if you feel uneasy or inadequate when not in their presence, you might need to deal with your own insecurities. Chronic feelings of loneliness are associated with feelings of low self-worth.[1]

The marriage relationship is significant: you are intertwined with your spouse and you reflect each other. Because marriage is an intense relationship, all that you experience together is amplified. Where there is joy, there is profound joy when shared in marriage. On the flip side, conflict is also augmented and can be more damaging to your wellbeing than similar disturbances with someone you care about less. Think about what happens when someone cuts you off on the freeway. It's a singular, fleeting moment of irritation, but you go your separate ways and forget about it pretty quickly. When your spouse cuts you off in conversation, however, you become irritated and don't go your separate ways. Not only that, but you remember similar interruptions from last week and last month. Because you are vulnerable with your spouse, the slight feels more personal.

Strong feelings and conflicts are normal, but dealing with them in a healthy way requires preparation. Recharging and refreshing ourselves with periods of time spent alone give us the energy we need to be engaged, patient and positive when we are together.

Time and Temperament

As much as Aminda and I enjoy each other's company, we both know that we can take too much of a good thing for granted, so we both have our own friends and interests outside of climbing. We have traveled separately as, well as together. We have no magic formula for the right amount of time to spend together—over the years we've struck a good balance based on our unique needs as a couple. We do know that our common interests create and reinforce our close bond.

We also know that the opposite is true: if a couple's purposes don't overlap at some point, the relationship is undermined. Entrepreneurs, for example, suffer a high divorce rate if they are the only spouse involved in the enterprise, because they tend to become married to their work and neglectful of their families. If the business is a joint venture, however, the partners have no time apart from each other between work and home, and their common purpose intensifies their bond.

Differences in temperament will also have an impact on the amount of time that couples need to be together or apart. For example, most of us can be described as either introverts or extroverts, which will determine how we refresh and recharge. Extroverts can spend time all day working and interacting with people, and then go home and relax by spending more time socializing. Introverts, on the other hand, can spend just as much time socializing but eventually need a little peace and quiet to recharge.

Couples need to be aware of each other's differences in temperament. The extrovert can't get offended when their introverted spouse disappears with a book for some down time. However, in order to be refreshed and present to their extroverted spouse during the day, the introvert might need to get up a few minutes early each morning for some time alone. Two introverts may not struggle to find alone time, but the fact that they are both comfortable being in the same room together without talking poses a different challenge: using that comfort as an excuse for not engaging in quality conversations and joint activities. On the other side of the continuum, two extroverts must take care to be present with each other when they are together, to listen to one another rather than talk over each other, and with an abundance of outside friends and commitments, it's quite possible that scheduling time together is a bigger problem than spending time apart.

Regardless of how much time they spend together or apart, spouses want to create enough space within their marriages to allow one another to "do their own thing." Managing this successfully begins with knowing themselves and each other. They need to communicate their needs to each other and be respectful of those needs. Using their valuable "me time" wisely, they can invest in activities and relationships that will nurture personal growth, which they can then reinvest in their marriages.

Developing Our Own Friendships

When romantic feelings for your partner first bubbled up, you were probably a little obsessed with every single detail about who they were and what made them tick. During dating and courtship, everything they said was new and fascinating, and you could spend hour upon hour in conversation. Now, years later, you definitely know your spouse. You've heard their jokes and stories several times. You can finish their sentences for them. The only thing you may want to know about them now is what they want for dinner, and let's be honest: you may not even care about the answer. Why do we feel like this sometimes? We can blame it on a sneaky thing called apathy. Luckily, there's a trick that can be used to fight it off: outside friendships.

Even though your spouse is your best friend, wholesome relationships outside marriage provide support and make you well-rounded people. Husbands and wives should encourage each other to maintain outside friendships. Getting together with others might require a little more coordination for married people than for singles, but it is worth the effort. Proverbs 27:10 advises us that we should "not forsake your friend or a friend of your family," (NIV) and Job 6:14 warns us that "anyone who withholds kindness from a friend forsakes the fear of the Almighty" (NIV).

Relationships and interests outside marriage allow us to learn new things and expand our experiences. We may end up with a nicer garden or better bowling score because of what we learn from outside activities, and the friends we make may also model "softer" skills, like how to forgive others or survive a crisis. As we grow, we can bring enriching skills, ideas and topics of conversation to our marriages. The late author and motivational speaker Jim Rohn said, "We become the combined average of the five people we associate most with."[2] The word "associate" indicates that we aren't required to know these people personally—only that we allow their influence to penetrate our thoughts.

Your spouse should there as one of those five people, but who else is in there? Family, friends, mentors and other people who positively contribute to our thoughts and experiences. Inclusion should be a big deal, should be earned—a result of trust developed over time. You can't always choose those with whom you interact, but you can choose whom you allow to influence you. The people closest to you will either pull you down or push you up. You want to ensure that your "top five" builds you up.

Love's True Test

John 15:13 says, "Greater love has no one than this: to lay down one's life for one's friends." Relating to this verse feels a little foreign. Really, how often are we asked to die for a friend? Mulling over that question is unpleasant. A circumstance in which we would be asked to choose between our own lives and a friend's is highly unlikely, so let's reword that verse in order to relate to it: "Greater love has no one than this: to stop what you are doing to help a friend in need." Our society is hyper-focused on "a life," on checking off a to-do list a mile long. When someone calls and asks for help, are we willing to drop what we're doing at the risk of completely messing up our schedules? (Okay, okay—some of us are probably *too* willing and are challenged by setting boundaries. If that's the case, it's wise to ask ourselves which of those friends are actually willing to set aside their lives when *we* need help.)

Surrounding ourselves with the right people may not "just happen." Friendships based on shared hobbies or vocations are convenient. We might need to seek out friendships based on faith. There is a special depth in friendships based on shared faith and a mutual relationship with God. It is these relationships that allow us to be vulnerable and transparent, and we need these friends in our inner circle.

Take Care with What We Share

Proverbs 27:9 says that "perfume and incense bring joy to the heart, and the pleasantness of a friend springs from their heartfelt advice" (NIV). Friends bring wisdom, council and a fresh perspective when we struggle to see beyond our own limited minds. Having trusted friends as prayer partners with whom we can share our hearts can be extremely beneficial to our marriages. Stormie Ormatian, author of both *The Power of a Praying Wife* and *The Power of a Praying Husband*, says, "I learned that the best thing for my marriage was for me to have women prayer partners with whom I prayed every week. I now believe this is vital for any marriage."[3]

As we share our hearts with friends, however, we don't have license to betray our spouses' confidence. We have no need to expose private details about our spouses or families. We may excuse such divulgences by telling ourselves that our friends need to understand how to counsel us or pray for us. Instead, we first protect our spouses' privacy then trust that God can give our friends insight about how to pray for us. If a private situation causes any of us to feel serious distress or helplessness, seeking counsel from a professional may be the best course of action.

As important as friends are, they cannot become more important than the marriage relationship. We can't treat our friends better than we do our spouses. Sometimes it seems easier for women to meet the emotional needs of their girlfriends by sending nice notes or complimenting an outfit. It can be more fun too, since women tend to make a big fuss about saying thank-you and giving compliments. And men, we that know a woman's needs can take some time and patience to figure out, but we have to let her know that she comes first in our lives—no matter what—because our spouses are always our first priority.

Draw Close to God

While your spouse comes first in your earthly life, marriage can't fill a spiritual void. The only way to cultivate a relationship with Christ is to spend time with Him in prayer and worship. Praying as a couple or with friends is powerful and awesome, but God also wants to share special, intimate moments with you in which you can be still and listen to Him.

Psalms 139 beautifully illustrates how close God is to us.

> You discern my going out and my lying down; you are familiar with all my ways. Before a word is on my tongue you, Lord, know it completely.... Where can I go from your Spirit? Where can I flee from your presence? . . . For you created my inmost being; you knit me together in my mother's womb . . . . Your eyes saw my unformed body; all the days ordained for me were written in your book before one of them came to be (3-16 NIV).

He wants us to draw close to him, to experience the intimacy with Him that He has made available to us. That starts when we are willing to "be still, and know that I am God" (Ps. 46:10). God wants us to express our hearts to Him—our hopes, desires and fears. When we pour ourselves out to Him, He fills us back up with His love and strength.

When we develop a relationship with Him, we learn to rely on Him, so He is where we run when trouble comes. One night in Idaho, Aminda and I were caught in a huge thunderstorm. Counting the seconds between thunder and lightning was nerve-racking; as the storm came closer and closer, it sounded as though we were in the middle of the thunder cloud. Lightning lit up our tent like a car's headlights. The thin nylon walls of our tent were keeping us dry, but they seemed insufficient to protect us from the rest of the storm. Psalms 91:1-2 gave us strength: "He who dwells in the secret place of the Most High Shall abide under the shadow of the Almighty. I will say of the Lord, He is my refuge and my fortress; My God, in Him I will trust." Knowing that our physical shelter was weak, we were happy that we could rest in the fortress of the Lord.

Whatever storms you are going through, the Lord will guard your heart if you draw near to Him. When you feel helpless and confused, His wisdom will be your guide. Similarly, when you don't understand something your spouse is dealing with, God can give you insight. Remember, marriage is two who have become one, and what happens to one happens to the other. You may naturally pray for yourself, to tell God your own needs, but if you aren't praying for your spouse, you're not maximizing the potential of that bond. Your prayers for them are powerful.

Freedom in His Presence

The best part about prayer is the freedom of expression it allows us. When we talk to people, we have so much to consider, from our words and expressions to our audience and the context of the conversation. When we talk to God, though, we don't need to craft the perfect message. Even when we don't understand our circumstances, when we don't know what we need or how to pray, God listens to our hearts and understands what we can't put into words. Exodus 2:24 says that "God heard their groaning and God remembered His covenant ...," and Mark 13:11 tells us not to "...worry beforehand about what to say. Just say whatever is given you at the time, for it is not you speaking, but the Holy Spirit" (NIV).

This is good news during times when we are angry, frustrated or confused by our spouses or our marriages—when we don't know what to say, what to do or how to feel, and when we don't know how to get unstuck and move forward. Alone in God's presence, we can scream and cry and release it all to His wise and understanding heart.

When your heart is right, your prayers invite God to exercise His power in your marriage. He can also provide powerful protection against attacks on your marriage if you boldly say, "I will not permit any plans of the enemy to prevail in our marriage." You can go ahead and ask God to do great things with your marriage. He wants to.

Psalms 32:7 says, "You are my hiding place; You will protect me from trouble and surround me with songs of deliverance" (NIV). When we draw close to God in a personal way, He blesses us. Whether in times of trouble or of peace, He wants to spend intimate time with each of us.

Summary

The intensity of the marriage relationship demands that we carve out time just to chill—when there aren't any issues to discuss, when we don't have to entertain, support or please one another. Such times give us space to develop outside interests, form friendships and grow spiritually.

While alone time doesn't always require being physically apart, it's important for couples not to become dependent on each other's presence for a sense of self. Feelings of insecurity or inadequacy when alone may indicate unresolved personal issues. We have to avoid shifting blame onto our spouses for not being physically present as much as we feel they need to be.

We don't want "tunnel vision" in our marriages, a state in which we get so wrapped up in our own irritations that we lose perspective. We need to step away and find some breathing room before a minor frustration becomes so large that we can't see beyond our own small world of hurt.

Even though our spouses are our best friends, relationships outside marriage provide support and make us well-rounded people. We should encourage and support each other's interests. Communication and attentiveness to each other's needs helps ensure the balance we need during time that we spend with our spouses.

RoadMap for Marriage

Questions for Reflection
1. Are you comfortable being alone?
2. Do you resent your spouse for not being physically present as much as you feel you need? Or do you feel you lack the space you need to chill?

Action Steps
1. Talk about your temperament similarities and differences and how this affects your need for more or less space.
2. Talk about ways you can encourage each other to develop outside friendships and activities.
3. Practice being alone in God's presence, and let His Spirit guide your prayers.

CHAPTER 10

FENDER-BENDERS HAPPEN
Practicing Forgiveness

As much as Josh and I love to travel, we're homebodies in the
sense that we really like our own space. Okay, maybe we're
really just control freaks. Whatever it is, we don't enjoy
crowded campgrounds, and it's not because we don't like the ranger to
tell us when we have to be quiet. No, we're the other guys, the boring
ones that quietly eat our dinner without a campfire and go to bed as
soon as it gets dark. For us, campgrounds can be challenging places, full
of unruly people.

Our aversion to campgrounds started soon after we were
married. We were on a climbing trip to Yosemite National Park. We
were anticipating camping in the low-priced, walk-in camp known
as Camp 4. Yosemite is a major destination for climbers from around
the globe, and Camp 4 is where they all connect. It has figured into

many legendary ascents as the place where partners met and big ideas germinated.

We certainly found Camp 4 buzzing with multicultural energy and brimming with youthful talent. Unfortunately, all of that energy manifested itself as noise and confusion outside of the posted quiet hours. Snuggled up in our sleeping bags on our first night there, we were jolted by the sounds of our Korean neighbors, who had returned well after dark from a full day. They barbequed up a storm, the clatter of dishes and hum of voices continuing until midnight, which wouldn't have been so painful if the German neighbors on our other side hadn't been up before dawn to start their day. It felt to us as though they were in and out of their tents and steel bear-boxes a hundred times before finally departing. The chorus of "ziiiiip, creeeeaaak, slam" roused us from dreamland.

Letting it Go

After that, we were more selective about our campsite choices, so we were happy to find one at a campground outside Lake Tahoe with mellow, friendly neighbors. They weren't around when we turned in one night, but all of a sudden they returned with a vengeance and with friends—all loud, drunk and still partying. We woke up immediately but popped in our earplugs and stayed calm—for a couple of hours. The noise was so close and so relentless that we couldn't rest. Finally, Josh had to make the dreaded move and confront them. The conversation went something like this:

Josh: "Hey guys, it's 1 a.m., and we're trying to sleep. Would you mind keeping it down?"

Drunk guy 20 feet away: "Hey, Man, we were just about to start the music. Why don't you come join us?"

Josh: "No thanks. Really, we'd just like to get back to sleep."

Drunk guy to his friends: "*#%!!@x!* I knew those guys were stiffs as soon as I saw them."

Drunk guy wasn't kidding around, and he immediately pulled out a guitar and launched in to some painfully bad tunes. By this time we were exhausted and emotional, but since we were wide awake, we talked over how to deal with the situation. First, we adjusted our climbing plans for the next day so we wouldn't overexert our fatigued selves. Then we decided to which campsite we would move. Even when the party finally dissipated, we were so tired and frustrated that we didn't feel that we'd ever calm down enough to sleep. That's when I (Aminda) had to do a little soul searching—praying, confessing my anger and asking for the wisdom to deal with it. The Word I received in response was "forgive."

"What?! Forgive those completely self-centered, obnoxious jerks?!"

"Yes, that's right."

"Okay, I guess I can give it shot. Lord, these people know not what they do." Somehow, saying it didn't feel good enough. ". . . and I forgive them—for invading our space, for interfering with our plans. God, I know that in the big picture, this is a trivial inconvenience and I will choose not to let it steal my joy."

Finally, three hours after our confrontation, the neighbors turned in, and we finally drifted back to sleep, only to wake with the sun at 7A.M. Despite our lack of sleep, I woke with a peaceful spirit after finally letting my anger go. The rude neighbors didn't win—Josh and I would enjoy the day in a beautiful place, no matter what.

Finding the Will to Forgive

We all know that forgiveness is of utmost importance in a marriage. We constantly have to let little things go—from the forgotten chore to that sarcastic comment. What we may not think about is how our external relationships can affect our marriages. Even when our anger or unforgiveness is directed towards someone else, that bitterness can have negative consequences in our domestic lives. It can alter our moods, infect our thoughts, distract us from finding joy and create barriers between us and our spouses.

We don't usually direct our anger towards drunk strangers. Unfortunately, we are more often irritated with coworkers, acquaintances or even family members whom we see on a regular basis, which makes ditching the attitude even more important. Otherwise, the grudge will fester and grow, making us more intolerant of irritations. Holding a grudge stops the flow of love, making a good relationship difficult.

Forgiveness takes effort. Instinctively, we want wrongs to be made right. When we spill something, we clean it up. When we break something, we fix it. That's just how the world works, so when we are wronged by others, we want them to make things right, and until they do, we feel disconcerted. We also feel hurt, angry or embarrassed, feelings which cloud our judgment and prevent us from seeing that we actually have the power to right the wrong ourselves by forgiving. Fostering an attitude of forgiveness takes commitment. And prayer. And practice. And more prayer.

Got to Have Grace

In Matthew 5:44, Jesus advises us to love our enemies and pray for those who persecute us. Now, it's easy to stop here and think something like, "Thank you, Jesus, for putting me in the United States, so I don't really get persecuted much."

But then He has to go and get personal.

"If you love those who love you, what rewards will you get? Do not even the tax collectors do the same? And if you greet your brethren only, what do you do more than others? Do not even tax collectors (pagans) do so?" (Mt. 5:46-47)

Sure, you love your spouse. You also have to live with them, so you forgive them, but apparently you also have to forgive the guy who cut you off on the freeway. And the colleague selected for the promotion that was supposed to be yours. And while you're not subject to the religious persecution referenced in the New Testament, this verse applies to anyone who has suffered abuse, theft or mistreatment. Forgiving such terrible injustices requires reliance on God.

If we continue reading in Matthew 5:48, we come to the command: "Be perfect, therefore, as your Father in heaven is perfect." Perfect ... seriously? That directive seems so impossible that we might just as well give up now, but Jesus didn't give us the command to set us up for failure. He left us with the gift of grace. Grace washes all our junk away and leaves us pure, or in other words, perfect. God says, "My grace is sufficient for you, for my strength is made perfect in weakness" (2 Cor. 12:9).

Receiving grace means understanding that a relationship with God is not contingent on our works. We don't grow closer to him based on accomplishing great things or avoiding pitfalls. Relying on our own ability to do right and reject wrong sets us up for failure, frustration and faltering faith. When we are too hurt or saddened even to think about forgiving, we can rely on God's power and grace to heal and restore our hearts. He tells us, "Come to me, all you who are weary and burdened, and I will give you rest. Take My yoke upon you ... and you will find rest for your souls. For My yoke is easy and My burden is light" (Mt. 11:28-30 NIV).

Persevere in Prayer

Cultivating an attitude of forgiveness does not mean we become doormats. Jesus chose His battles wisely, but He wasn't spineless. He was tough, and He demonstrated that we can be tough, strong and assertive, yet totally loving and forgiving at the same time. I (Josh) stood up for both Aminda and me when I spoke the truth to our campground neighbors. However, I was respectful; I didn't sink to their level by insulting them or using harsh language (though I may have wanted to).

The process of forgiveness transforms us from being victims of someone else's behavior into people with the courage to persevere.[1] We're made strong in perseverance, but not in aggressiveness. Our hearts are softened in humility, not passiveness.

Jesus told us to pray for those who mistreat us. He understood that this can be a challenging command, so he gave us an effective starting point when He prayed, "Father, forgive them, for they know not what they do" (Luke 23:34).

Finding His Peace

Sometimes we are insulted because we assume that an offender is truly "out to get us," that they know darn well they are being selfish, rude, inconsiderate jerks, but just don't care enough to stop. In reality, they have moved on, while we allow their transgressions to fester and grow. Like a rock hitting a car windshield, the initial hit is hard and the crack it creates is deep. The car owner can choose to take the wound seriously, react quickly and have it filled to prevent more damage, or leave it and allow the crack to grow. If left unchecked, the damage threatens to destroy the window. We can't rely on the offender to give us the closure we need; rather we repair the damage ourselves through forgiveness.

We're all human and at some point have unintentionally said or done something insensitive. Do we set out with a mission to be offensive? No. But we all make mistakes and we all need forgiveness. We know how it feels to cause hurt, so we can also understand how terrible others may feel when they are responsible for our pain, even if they don't show it.

We really do have to say, "Father, *I* forgive them, for they know not what they do." We can even continue with a prayer that the offenders' hearts will be softened and that any hurts of their own will be healed.

And what if we can't shake vengeful thoughts of their getting hurt and not healed? Well, God helps us out with that, too. "Do not take revenge, my dear friends, but leave room for God's wrath, for it is written: 'It is mine to avenge; I will repay, says the Lord' " (Rom.12:19 NIV). We can be honest with God about our desire to seek retribution—He understands that tendency in us. Just as we can cast all our cares on Him, we can release to Him a desire for revenge. We can free ourselves from it before it leads to sin and regret. Only when we stop wishing for revenge on those who offend us will we know the peace of having truly forgiven them.

Forgiveness and Low Self-Esteem

A difficulty forgiving may point to low self-esteem. When we rely on God, not others, for our self-worth, we don't need others to make us feel good about ourselves, meaning we aren't as quick to take offense. With a healthy sense of self, we are more inclined to give others the benefit of the doubt and to let offenses slide. We also realize that we are extending to others what God has extended to us. We have the power to do this because "… the Spirit who lives in you is greater than the spirit who lives in the world" (1 John 4:4).

Finding peace is hard when we are easily offended. Our relationships are affected when we fear that others are laughing and talking about us. That's why we can't take everything so personally. When we hear something that touches a nerve, we have two choices: we can react in the flesh and get hurt feelings, or we can have the maturity and confidence to move on. Even if the offense is personal, sometimes we just have to assume that it was unintentional and recognize that people make mistakes. We can't change what was done or the people who hurt us.

More important, we can't let anything that hurt us is in the past steal a single minute from the future.

When we struggle to reach the point of forgiveness, it may indicate unresolved insecurities. Often, insecurity is a symptom of pride—an attitude that we deserve respect from others or that they owe us something, like an apology. In essence, we're deciding how our offenders should pay for their offenses. However, judging others and doling out punishment is not our role on this earth. God is the only judge, and His judgment goes beyond justice. He's judged all of us as equally undeserving of the forgiveness He freely offered. We are all saved by grace.

Yes, an apology might feel good, but forgiving feels even better. Forgiving others can actually help us improve our self-esteem, which makes it easier to forgive the next time. Healthy self-esteem is not developed as much by receiving compliments and affirmations as it is by behaving in ways that we find worthy of our own respect. Forgiving others fits that category.

Forgive Thyself

When we are really challenged to let something go, we want to acknowledge that challenge. Sometimes, the harder we try to pretend something doesn't matter, the more it upsets us. The solution begins with confronting our feelings, being honest about what specifically caused the hurt and why it matters so much. Forcing ourselves to dig deep and think logically about our feelings will allow us to move beyond raw emotion. Do the feelings follow a pattern in our lives? Is there someone or something in the past that we haven't forgiven?

We may find that we're having trouble forgiving ourselves. When we don't think we're worthy of forgiveness, we often try to punish ourselves. Just as we can't love others until we love ourselves, we can't show mercy to others when we are harshly self-critical of our own faults or past behaviors. Fortunately, Romans 5:20 tells us that where sin increased, grace increased all the more. His grace is abundant and sufficient. We need to receive it, give thanks for it and move on. Our sinful natures were buried with Christ so that we may live new lives.

God has an abundance of love and forgiveness for us if we come to Him with an open heart. By accepting His forgiveness, we receive the freedom to walk in His will because we want to, because His presence compels us to. God wants our focus to be on Him, not on our sin. We have to let go of those things in our past—whatever causes us to feel unworthy of forgiveness—for which we can't forgive ourselves. There is no reason to keep mentally flogging ourselves. If we don't stop trying to erase past sins and behaviors by being perfect in the present and the future, we risk becoming impossibly critical, both of ourselves and of the families we represent.

The more we are preoccupied with avoiding sin, the harder it becomes to avoid it, and dwelling on past mistakes makes repeating them more likely. God doesn't want us to live like that—He makes our yokes easy and our burdens light.

Forgive Your Heritage

Many factors make us who we are, but the largest influence on what we become is family. As we make peace with who we are and what we've done, we also need to make peace with our families. Even if we largely admire our heritage, most of us would like to leave other parts of it in the past. We can do that in either a healthy or unhealthy way. The unhealthy way is, unfortunately, the most instinctive way to go about leaving our pasts behind—we tend to view it as a problem to solve and focus all our attention on it on fixing it. We attack our pasts with steely resolve and definitive promises to ourselves: "I will never make my children sit at table until they have finished their vegetables." "I will never let my husband be in control of our finances."

Our intentions may be completely positive, but this approach is ineffective. First, all of our resolute energy is focused on the negative—the hurt and frustration that we are trying to forget—which reinforces the past because we focus on negative memories. Second, we're not dealing with the core issue of unforgiveness. If we were the ones who had to sit miserably at the dinner table until bedtime, if we witnessed a grandmother struggling to gain access to her widow's bank account, we took those experiences as personal insults. Whether it was we who suffered or someone in our lineage, our steely resolve not to let it happen again focuses on negative experiences.

A more effective way to deal with family scars starts with forgiveness. We can begin by acknowledging that our parents and grandparents did the best they could with what they had and knew at the time. Could they have become tired, lazy and discouraged at times, and did they have some momentary lapses in judgment? Absolutely. As parents, so will we.

It's too easy to say things like, "If my parents had encouraged me to go to college, I would be better off financially." "If my parents had supported my desire to attend cosmetology school, I would be happier." "If my parents hadn't gotten a divorce, I wouldn't have such a hard time making my marriage work." We may never know exactly what was at the core of our parents' decisions—what they were thinking or feeling or going through—but asking them, listening to them and learning from them may be valuable in helping us empathize and understand. In any case, it doesn't matter. The best response is forgiveness—and to receive healing from the ultimate Healer.

We can choose our friends and we can choose our spouses, but we cannot choose our families, so the only option is to make peace with who we are and where we came from. That means embracing the positive and releasing the negative, setting our futures free from the past.

The Jealousy Trap

A hindrance to making peace with our families can be the feeling that we're the only ones who need to do so, that everyone else has it easier than we do. This feeling reveals how unforgiveness can create sneaky problems. We may not even realize that we have to forgive others for having things that we want. When we resent others for their successes or advantages, we have succumbed to jealousy or covetousness. God strongly warns us against it, because He knows that jealousy can create heavy burdens and mess up relationships. We are told that "a heart at peace gives life to the body, but envy rots the bones" (Prov. 14:30 NIV). Envy burdens our souls with discontent, the opposite of peace and happiness.

The good news is that we can still want things. Jealousy and envy are what we throw away. Aminda and I want a lot of things. While on the road, for example, we really, really wanted one of those cool Sportsmobiles, which we think are the ultimate camping vehicles—more compact than a trailer or an RV, but more durable and convenient than a tent. Equipped with 4-wheel drive and a lifted suspension, they could take us to some cool camp sites, so we always gawked at the ones we passed. We didn't, however, resent the people who owned and drove them. Jealousy says, "That's not fair. Why do other people have such cool camper vans when we just have a tent?" We took on a different attitude. We decided to believe that we were drawn to the Sportsmobile for a reason: there will be one in our future. Since then we've been saving and preparing to buy one.

Keep Believing

We can't confuse envy with dreams or desires to achieve goals and to obtain assets. Envy or resentment—feelings of perceived lack when compared to others—can be damaging to a relationship. We can't blame our spouses for the lack of something we covet. "If he would just work harder and get that promotion …." "If he hadn't sunk so much money in a new business …." "If she didn't spend so much money on shoes, we might have a bigger house or be able to take nicer vacations." Such thoughts are never productive.

Envy isn't always focused on material objects. How often do women envy the "super-mom" who seems to do it all perfectly—family, career, relationships—and look perfect, too? How often do men covet the promotion that comes with respect, bonuses and a nice, big office? At some point, we all experience envy in one form or another. Aminda and I sometimes feel envious of people who are stronger climbers than we are. It often seems as though they just have more natural ability than we do, even though we know that they work and train hard.

Anyone who has dealt with chronic illness or injury certainly battles envy towards those who are healthy and unburdened, as I am well aware. After several years of riding and racing mountain bikes in college and completing the Great Divide Trail (2100 miles through four states in 54 days), my knees rebelled. I could no longer enjoy the activities I loved without knee pain.

Through the next season of my life, my range of motion was limited when hiking and climbing, and I nearly had to avoid mountain biking altogether. I battled my emotions during this time: this injury really didn't seem fair; I believed in God as the Divine Healer, so why was God continuing to let me live for so many years with this pain? I knew that plenty of people biked as much or more than I had without so much suffering. Why me?

I never stopped believing and never sat idly by, expecting God to send a lightning bolt of healing simply because I thought I deserved it. I researched, prayed, sought prayer from others and went to medical specialists…until finally one of them had the remedy I needed. (Amen!)

Envy is rooted in fear—fear that we won't get what we deserve, or that we're not worthy of much because of past sins. During trials and tribulations, envy can create a crippling root of bitterness and discontent in the core of our spirits. As with any other negative thought, we must recognize it as an unproductive attitude and replace it with positive thoughts that bring the opposite of turmoil, which is peace. When we are content with who we are, where we are and what we have, peace follows.

Summary

Forgiveness is especially crucial in maintaining a healthy marriage. Forgiveness brings the peace and harmony that we all want in our homes. Without it we are left with strife and discord. Forgiveness requires commitment and practice. If we are unable to forgive ourselves or others, we will find it more difficult to forgive our spouses. Unforgiveness keeps us in the past; forgiveness keeps us present and grounded.

Unforgiveness burdens relationships. We can't feel close, personal connections with either God or our spouses when we are angry and self-centered. Unforgiveness damages our ability to love, because love can't live alongside resentment. A heart is full of love has no room for bitterness.

Forgiveness brings release from bitterness, softens our hearts and brings us peace. That means we intentionally choose forgiveness, just as we choose other positive thoughts. When we liberate others from their wrongs, we also release ourselves from the hurt resulting from offense.

RoadMap for Marriage

Questions for Reflection

1. Can you identify old baggage that is weighing down your marriage? What steps can you take to lighten the load?

2. Do you truly believe that God's mercies are new every morning, that He will forgive you and give you the gift of a fresh start? Choose today to accept this gift.

Action Steps

1. Practice calming yourself down when anger or pain from the past resurfaces. Look for small ways to practice forgiveness each day.
2. Commit to saying a daily prayer for someone who has offended you.

CHAPTER 11

CAUTION, STEEP CURVES AHEAD

Speaking the Truth in Love

A great thing about mountain biking is that almost anyone can hop on a bike and enjoy a trail ride, because mountain bikes are equipped with the good brakes, comfortable suspension, wide tires and good traction that rough, uneven surfaces demand. Even an inexperienced rider can roll over small roots and rocks almost effortlessly. Those small obstacles allow a rider to practice rudimentary skills before they encounter larger obstacles requiring balance and technique.

Similarly, God has perfectly equipped us to coast through the small obstacles we encounter in our marriages. We hardly notice the minor frustrations. We can handle them effortlessly because He has equipped us with the fruit of the Spirit, which includes love and patience. Small disagreements allow us to practice the communication and conflict resolution skills that we'll need to handle more complicated difficulties.

We know that life's big obstacles will come our way. Prayer and optimism will always help us endure the storms within marriage, but they won't prevent them.

The fact is, we live in a fallen world, which means that we face challenging, melancholy days as well as peaceful, joyful ones. Without this range of experience, life would be pretty bland. The variations of life keep us engaged. If we merely went through the same motions day after day, we would eventually check out and stop investing ourselves in our daily activities. But we don't live like that. Instead, we engage with others and share ourselves, which makes us vulnerable and puts us at risk of getting hurt. Without fail, we all eventually face less than perfect circumstances.

Variety is good—we need it in daily life, just as Aminda and I do in mountain biking. Sure, we could ride a flat, straight trail for miles and miles, but after a while we would be bored. When we ride up a long, steep hill, on the other hand, we get uncomfortable. Our legs hurt, our lungs burn, our heads ache and our mouths are dry. What we can't feel, though, is the chemical reactions induced by our effort. During hard climbs, our bodies manufacture endorphins, peptides which produce a sense of euphoria. Riding downhill is always fun, but riding downhill after an endorphin-producing uphill ride is especially exhilarating. The hard climb enhances the reward.

Climbing a steep hill within marriage may make your head and heart hurt, but it also offers an opportunity to dig deep and share things with each other that may not have surfaced before. It requires you to rely on one another more and to tackle seriously difficult problems together. When it's all over (and it *will* end), when the sweet relief of a lifted burden arrives, you can hold one another and celebrate victory together. You will know each other in a deeper way and will look at each other with more respect, having seen each other's strong, courageous side.

Riding Through the Bumps

In mountain biking, the only way to become skilled at negotiating obstacles is to practice. A rider can choose either to walk around a big obstacle or to take the risk of riding through it. Riders who really want to improve will not only attempt it once, but will turn around and ride through the obstacle again and again until it gets easy, knowing that the best way to be successful in tough situations is to practice.

When we encounter conflict in marriage, especially early on, it's tempting to walk around and avoid it. It seems easier to play nice and tiptoe around our partners' feelings. Instead, we want to face conflict, examine its cause and deal with it. We have no reason to fear or avoid disagreement. Marital conflict is inevitable, but the outcome does not have to be negative. It can provide opportunities to think harder, to be more creative, to develop greater understanding and to search for alternative and more effective avenues of communication. Unresolved conflict, however, can break a team down and be costly to a relationship.

Engaging in conflict may be uncomfortable because it produces changes. Arriving at a positive outcome requires time and commitment to work through differences—differences of opinion, personality, style and points of view—which can provide an impetus for creative problem solving.

Conflict is healthy as long as it is handled effectively. By addressing conflict thoughtfully, we increase the likelihood of becoming more accepting of our spouses' beliefs, perspectives and experiences. Conflict resolution is an ongoing process for couples, and we have to be confident in our ability to transform it into something healthy and productive. Once we have experienced the benefits of dealing with conflict, i.e. increased trust, a stronger bond, and more open communication, we learn to face conflict willingly rather than avoid it.

Encourage Engagement

In any popular campground or national park, visitors are guaranteed to find some pretty fat and happy wildlife. Caught up in the excitement of being surrounded by nature, tourists use food as a way to lure the cute little squirrels and rabbits close enough for a photo opportunity. As a result, the animals are free from the effort normally required to hunt or forage for food. They may look fat and healthy, but being fed by humans actually upsets their natural balance. They become overpopulated, more vulnerable to disease and less wary about the danger of vehicles.

We don't want to become too fat and happy in our marriages, either, by taking a passive, disinterested approach. Marriage requires attention. We want to be engaged and interested in what's happening, even if it is unpleasant. Avoiding conflict can create surface-level contentment and short-term happiness, but it isn't healthy in the long run. Instead, learning how to deal with conflict in a healthy way will leave our marriages stronger than before. Small bumps along the way are useful for training so that we can climb hills together and tackle bigger rocks head-on rather than go around them. If we embrace challenges, we come out victorious on the other side.

Conflict stems from different interests and needs. Usually, those differences are like small bumps: easily resolved. What turns small bumps into bigger obstacles? Sometimes an external or extreme circumstance— illness, poverty or loss—heightens emotions and makes disagreements more difficult. However, difficult circumstances also have the potential to bring a couple closer together. The most common culprit behind serious strife is selfishness.

Stubborn pride and selfishness will prevent us from resolving marital conflicts. Eventually you will need something from marriage that isn't forthcoming, or your spouse will have to ask something of you. When that time comes, you want to cultivate an attitude of compromise, because a soft and flexible heart is required to work through tough disagreements.

Communicating During Conflict

Compromise isn't effective unless both parties are willing to express their individual needs. If we don't, eventual resentment and a lack of fulfillment can cause big problems. Expressing our needs incorrectly can also cause big problems, as we may be misinterpreted, so how on earth can we get it right? The answer can be found in Ephesians 4:15, which instructs us to speak the truth in love. There is tremendous wisdom in those five words. When we face disagreements with love, we release all negative attitudes toward our spouses. We tell the truth not out of selfish desire but because we know that it will be better for our marriages and better for each of us as individuals.

When speaking the truth in love, you can say things that your spouse doesn't want to hear but needs to hear. If your heart is in the right place, if you have genuine, Spirit-filled love for your spouse, the way you present yourself should be evident: you choose your words carefully and then speak them gently and lovingly.

James 1:19 advises us to be "quick to listen, slow to speak and slow to become angry" (NIV). When we know that our spouses are speaking in love, we find it easy to trust them. When we are on the receiving end of truth that is hard to swallow, we can stomach the medicine because it is dispensed with a spoonful of sugary affection.

While on an expedition in the Antarctic, Deborah and Rolf Shapiro lived isolated from civilization for nine months, having no one for company but each other. Their seclusion required humility, open-mindedness and putting the team's needs ahead of the individual's. When Rolf pointed out a circumstance which was causing Deborah to act more aggressively, she accepted his feedback. "Then," she explains, "whenever I felt the anger, I would simply keep my mouth shut." The Shapiros had to remain sensitive to each other's moods and concerns, never belittling one another. At the end of it, the couple not only endured the challenge of seclusion but strengthened their marriage through it.[1]

Calmly accepting the truth can be difficult. We may get angry, sad, hurt and embarrassed, all at the same time, and we may feel the need to express all our crazy thoughts and emotions. Generating a calm response in an intense situation requires a healthy amount of self-control. Choosing to stay cool and collected is related to self-efficacy, a person's sense of being in control. People with well-developed self-efficacy believe that no matter what life throws at them, they can choose their reactions and decisions which in turn shape their lives. People with poorly developed self-efficacy, on the other hand, tend to see their lives as outside their control. Needless to say, those with well-developed self-efficacy are better able to hear hard truth and accept it, because they understand that they are in control of their responses.

Keeping our Cool

How do we develop self-efficacy? We can do it in several ways, but one of the most effective is to practice. We can practice keeping the tone of our voices calm and rational, even when we feel like exploding with anger. An awareness of our emotions and reactions during difficult exchanges is important, too; armed with an understanding of how we react, we can effectively regulate feelings of stress during challenging discussions. Self-regulation is a form of healthy self-control, and practicing self-control develops self-efficacy.

Another way to develop self-efficacy is to observe and emulate desired behaviors in others. You can seek out and spend time with the people in your life who have admirable marriages. You can also watch movies and television programs featuring positive relationships, turning off the shows with dysfunctional role models.

Any choice affecting your well-being, from flossing your teeth to exercising regularly, requires some degree of self-efficacy. The degree to which your self-efficacy is developed influences how you set and achieve goals. It determines how much effort you will expend and how long that effort will be sustained in the face of obstacles and failures. In general, people with high self-efficacy are more likely to put effort into to accomplishing tasks and to persist longer in those efforts.

Self-efficacy isn't about control—it's about cultivating the attitude that life isn't determined by what's thrown at you. Healthy self-efficacy leads conscious choices about your response to circumstances. It influences the ways in which you utilize positive conditions and deflect negative ones. Controlling your response to difficult situations enhances communication with your spouse. You're better able to swallow tough words, to remain calm and cool when feeling hurt and confused, and to respond lovingly.

And in those times when our spouses don't express themselves very lovingly? Well, self-control is even more valuable. When they get riled up and give us some attitude, we can choose to stay cool and collected. We all know that it takes two people to fight, so if one person remains calm instead of firing back, the other person won't have anyone to fight with. This can keep a heated discussion from becoming too hot to handle.

Getting to the Root of Conflict

Even though we are wise to refuse a fight, we don't want to ignore underlying issues. The root cause of a spouse's emotional and confrontational attitude may be a legitimate concern. When we choose to look beyond emotional displays, we often find truth. When we let our spouses know that we are willing to listen but will not take the bait to engage in a fight, we give them time to calm down and find a better way to express their needs.

Pent up feelings lead to passive-aggressive behavior; negative feelings always "leak" in ways that confuse and frustrate our spouses. However, this doesn't mean that it's acceptable to lash out and spew ugly words. Feelings are best expressed rationally and maturely.

Men especially want to realize that when a wife airs her feelings, it is usually an act of love. For women, emotional expression is a way of engaging in healthy communication, not a personal attack. Women know that when grievances simmer without release, they eventually boil over, and they may find it helpful to point this out to their husbands before engaging in a difficult conversation. It is also helpful for women to center the conversation very specifically on the behavior that is upsetting them. Vague generalizations may strike their husbands as criticism of who they are rather than what they are doing.

Men are automatic problem solvers, which can be frustrating to wives who just want their husbands to listen. Aminda has certainly experienced some intense emotions while rock climbing, from fear to frustration to exhaustion, and has had to find ways to let me know what her needs are in difficult moments. I am ten inches taller than she is. I have long limbs, so the sequences of movement that I use to climb a route are usually much different from the ones she uses during an ascent. There are times when she comes to a really tough move. She finds herself uncomfortable, tired, frustrated and confused about how to make progress. I don't like to see Aminda upset and uncomfortable, so in those situations my instinct is to help her out by telling her where to put her hands. More than once, her response to my good-natured help has been a very ungrateful shout: "I... can't... REACH that far!"— maybe with a "Duh, I'm not six feet tall!" or "Just leave me alone, you're not helping!" tacked on for good measure. So, I have learned to limit my offers of help to something more generic like "Keep breathing, you're doing great, Babe!"

On the other hand, there are times when she really does need my help. Finding herself without a necessary piece of gear can be a safety issue, not just a personal frustration. If she allowed herself to become flustered and burst into tears, I wouldn't know how to help her figure out what knot to tie or what to use as a backup. In cases like this, she has learned that she needs to take a deep breath, calm down and say, "Babe, I'm not sure what to do. Can you help me figure it out?" She knows that she needs to listen to me and respect my answer rather than get angry and upset.

During a conflict, the emotion most likely to cause trouble is anger. Anger itself is neither bad nor sinful. Because we are Christ-followers, we're totally justified in being upset over sin. Evils such as abuse or racism should incense us. The anger directed toward injustice is the same anger that spurs us to right the wrong. Unfortunately, most people confuse anger with losing their tempers, and it's that loss of control that causes sin. That's why Ephesians 4:26 says "in your anger do not sin" (NIV).

Manage Anger, Manage Conflict

Anger is another one of those emotions that can be rooted in self-esteem. It is often triggered by insult, rude treatment or a sense of danger—not only by threats to our physical well-being, but also by threats to our pride or dignity. In response, we instinctively react with a fight-or-flight response.[2]

Once we pull the initial trigger, we're either on the offensive or defensive, and anger can quickly consume us. Pulling the trigger again heightens our emotions further, and whether our anger is a passive flight or an aggressive fight, it can build and escalate until we erupt emotionally.

Suppressing anger is not the better option; it can actually prolong a heightened emotional state and result in an even bigger outburst. It's no wonder that anger is the emotion that puts us most at risk for cardiac problems—all that tension decreases the efficiency of the heart.[3]

There are healthy ways of dealing with anger. The earlier we deescalate our anger, the better our chances to avoid an outburst. This means that when we are angry with our spouses, we must pause and deal with it before attempting to resolve the conflict. Once we have reined in our anger, we then need to ask ourselves what is underneath and why our reactions are so intense. Spousal disagreements can generate overwhelming emotions and trigger strong fight-or-flight responses. After all, much is at stake in marriage, including some of our most fundamental needs.

When we are angry and engaged in conflict, we may subconsciously fear losing love or being abandoned by our spouses. Deep down, we fear those things and recognize the risk of experiencing them. We react by trying to protect ourselves—either by fighting the threat head-on or by running away and ignoring it.

Press On

Disagreements often have less to do with the issue at hand than with our underlying emotions. When our spouses disagree with us, could our anger be the result of feeling that they aren't listening to us, supporting us or respecting us? By asking that question, we might realize that anger is not about the other person, but is a secondary reaction to something deeper, like hurt or jealousy. Once we have come to such a realization, we can challenge the emotion. We can ask ourselves if our reaction was really about the present conflict or more about something in the past that remains unresolved. If we discover that it is the latter, we let our spouses off the hook. At the very least, we can try to see the situation from the other person's perspective and refocus our energies on being empathic and compassionate.

A cooling down period, such as a long walk, can be effective as long as the time is not spent feeding angry thoughts. Distractions such as movies can be useful as well, as long as they are pleasant and not upsetting. Venting, however, usually does not work. Rather than diffusing volatile emotions, venting continually revisits the situation, which just prolongs anger. Cooling down and settling differences in a constructive manner are much healthier.

A way to instill ourselves with constructive responses to negative situations is to focus on being optimistic. Optimists see failure as a stepping stone to success. Pessimists view failure as part of their character and see themselves as helpless to change. We know that we are neither incapable of improvement, helpless to change our circumstances nor enslaved to our emotions.

We also know that personal growth requires work and discipline. We can use professional athletes as examples. They may love their sports and competition, but they do not get up every single day excited about the long hours of hard work ahead of them. They endure bad weather, fatigue or plain old feelings of laziness. To succeed, they have to be tougher than the forces working against them. They know that the only things separating them from the competition are commitment and perseverance. They can't control the rain, but they can control the way they respond to it. They focus on the result: the cheers of the crowd, the winning moment. In the same way, we can commit to the goal of a winning relationship. We have to rise above momentary anger and frustration, and press on towards the joy of restoration.

Enlisting Support

Anger can give us major tunnel vision. We can get so wrapped up in our own irritations that we lose perspective. What begins as a minor frustration can so consume us that we can't see beyond our own small world of hurt. To break free, we might need a fresh perspective from a third party who can tell us that we're over-reacting, under-reacting or not considering an important detail.

In preparation for tough times, it is wise to consider the support networks that we currently have in place. What couples, family members or church groups do we admire and trust? Who models the healthy communication that we seek in our own marriages?

Just as being a child of divorce does not destine us to suffer the same fate, being raised in a conflict-filled environment doesn't require that we accept the same for our own adult lives. Even if we feel ill-equipped to deal with anger because of our childhood environments, or even if we have never observed healthy communication, it is never too late to find new role models. We can choose people whom we admire and want to emulate. We can commit to spending time with them and learn from their behavior. We can enlist their help, and let them offer wisdom, insight and accountability.

If we share feelings about our marriages, it is best to do so with someone who will keep our conversations in confidence. People in whom we confide should be willing to spend as much time listening as required before drawing wise conclusions and giving us the honest perspective that we need.

Speaking the truth in love extends beyond the words we speak *to* our spouses. In times of conflict, when we may be hurt or angry, speaking negatively *about* them does nothing to make the situation better. Our support systems are not for complaining about our marriages, but for making ourselves better so that we can become better husbands or wives.

Make a Move

No matter what, remember that we determine the outcome of our lives and our marriages. We cannot allow the past to dictate our future. Sure, we'll make mistakes, say hurtful things or forget something important, but we want to remain committed to producing positive results. When we cross the line into feelings of helplessness, we make the recovery from challenges much more difficult.

When ascending big mountains, hikers may face what's called a false summit. A hiker sets his sight on a distant peak that appears to be the end of their journey, only to arrive and find another peak still above. The route there might be narrow, rocky and steep. It might feel daunting after coming so far already. A mountain may have multiple false summits, which can play tricks with a hiker's mind, clouding his judgment with disappointment and doubt. When arriving at a false summit a hiker wants to rest. Instead, he has to dig deep inside to find the energy to press on. The hiker has to take a deep breath, put one foot in front of the other and keep going.

Sometimes life is like that, too. In our minds, resolution can seem discouragingly out of reach, but if we simply stand up and commit to putting one foot in front of the other, we often find we can reach the place of peace and rest that we seek.

Personal support is sometimes the best technique to use for a grasp on clarity, to show us that rest is within our reach. God doesn't want us to travel through life alone. When your spouse feels distant, He can come along side you and work through others—church leaders or mentors—to help you carry your burdens. You never need to be too scared or too proud to ask for help.

Catch God's Vision

During tough times we can hold fast to God's vision of marriage. When negative emotions are so overwhelming that we feel suffocated and can't see past our difficulties, we have to reach our hands towards the One who can see the bigger picture—the past, present and future. Through Him we see the unseen. He sees a troubled present as the blink of an eye in comparison to the amazing future that He wants to give us. In Him we have hope for a better tomorrow.

Scripture tells us that God is in the business of restoration. "I will restore to you the years that the swarming locust has eaten" (Joel 2:25 NIV). We can trust Him to take away the pain, hopelessness, hardness, and unforgiveness that we may have endured in our marriages. He is able to resurrect love and life from the deadest of places.

When we realize that we are facing the sickness, poverty or "for worse" with which the world challenges marriage, when we realize that our relationships have suffered a serious blow, we have to believe that the relationship can be restored, says author Stormie Ormartian. "Know that whatever has crept into our relationship, selfishness or apathy can be removed. We have to trust that God is big enough to accomplish all this and more. God's will is to heal wounds and put love back in your heart. But you have to be humble enough to let him— willing to take off the armor you've put up to protect yourself, even if that leaves you feeling vulnerable and insecure."[4] God can make anyone a new creation. We can't write off a marriage until we've fought for it through prayer, because as long as we are praying, there is hope.

Summary

Any time we share ourselves, we become vulnerable enough to risk getting hurt. The interconnected relationship between spouses produces strong feelings of both love and fear. The fear of disappointing or losing such an important person is usually at the root of anger.

We don't want to get too fat and happy in marriage, nor can we afford to take a passive, disinterested approach to our spouses. Marriage requires attention. We want to be engaged and interested in what's happening.

If our spouses become disengaged, pulling them back might require tough conversations. God has given us simple instructions for having those conversations: we are to speak the truth in love. If our hearts are in the right place, if we have genuine, Spirit-filled love for our spouses, we'll choose our words carefully and then communicate them gently and lovingly.

If our spouses haven't been speaking in love, or if outside circumstances are causing strain, we can always remember that what's thrown at us isn't as important as how we respond to it. We can allow ourselves to acknowledge pain and feel our emotional reactions. Then we actively seek hope in God's promises for a better tomorrow. During times when we've lost our own vision of the marriage we planned, we can hold fast to God's vision of marriage.

RoadMap for Marriage

Questions for Reflection

1. Do you have deep-rooted hurts, fears or anger that you haven't dealt with? Do you need to seek professional assistance?
2. What causes you to become angry at your spouse? Can you identify any pride at the root of that anger?
3. What can you do today to hone the self-efficacy that will help you weather tomorrow's challenges?

Action Steps

1. Talk to your spouse about your relationship fears. Discuss your feelings about divorce, how that affects your reaction to conflict and your vision of your life together.
2. Talk about each other's differences. Consider who your spouse is, where he/she came from, what experiences shaped what he/she is and does today.

CHAPTER 12

TAKING THE SCENIC ROUTE
Quality Time over Quantity

Given our love of travel, it's no surprise that both Josh's parents and mine have one thing in common: they enjoy nice, scenic drives with awe-inspiring vistas, gorgeous landscapes and plenty of photography stops. Unlike a commute to work, scenic drives aren't about arriving at a destination on time. The whole idea is to travel slowly enough to enjoy the view. It doesn't matter how long or short the drive is; it just matters that the route is beautiful. There is something special about taking time to appreciate and admire our surroundings.

Marriage should be more like a scenic drive than a commute to work. Time with each other shouldn't always be focused on a certain destination, like keeping a perfect house or raising a perfect family. I don't want to feel as though I'm clocking in and out of a job, logging enough time to earn my title of wife. We can't engage marital cruise control and zone out, either, failing to appreciate each other.

Josh and I definitely didn't lack for time together on our road trip. If quantity time had been our goal we would be wearing gold medals, but spending all that time together in silence—or worse, in conflict—would not have nurtured our relationship. If our goal had simply been quantitative, we could have missed a once-in-a-lifetime opportunity to connect on a deeper level. Sure, our activities and means of travel required us to communicate, but we also took advantage of long hours in the car. When we could have sat in silence, we chose instead to open up and share our dreams, ambitions, fears and joys.

Remember Deborah Shapiro, who spent nine months in a confined space in Antarctica with no one but her husband? She explains that one key to harmony was the purposeful scheduling of time alone. She and her husband had to give each other freedom and space, which, she found, required consideration and restraint. "One has to be able to give the other person 'mental elbow room,' " she explains. "During our winter, when a person settled into the sofa in the salon with a book and started reading, he or she was not interrupted. Keeping quiet when the person is close enough to practically read one's thoughts, is a matter of self-discipline, fuelled by caring."[1]

Then, when they were back together—they were engaged, which was key to avoiding the restlessness that fuels frustration and conflict. "Showing tangible signs of caring and of empathy ensures that cabin fever never takes hold," explains Deborah. The couple shared responsibility for being enjoyable company, planning and demonstrating enthusiasm for the games, reading and discussions that they used to unwind after the day's work. "One can only be as bored as one is boring," says Deborah.

Quality Communication

Being enjoyable company requires being present and engaged, and being engaged means participating in both sharing and listening. We all know that listening is an important part of communication and relationship building, but given the hectic pace most of us keep, it's a skill that often isn't honed.

According to leadership expert, Steven Covey, we often use dysfunctional listening practices, or "shortcuts," to cope with our busy lifestyles. While our partners are talking, we may be formulating our responses before we've heard them out, just so there's no awkward pause. Or we keep one ear on the TV and listen just enough to hear what we want or to offer a cursory response. Sometimes we cut through the small talk or formalities and spew out a string of courtroom-style questions so that our partners will get right to the point. Then, instead of asking clarifying questions for better understanding, we jump in and respond with a story of our own.

Unfortunately, most of us engage in one or more of these ineffective listening habits. Honing your listening skills may mean slowing down. You may have to listen to things you've heard before or things that don't interest you. Good listening requires patience and practice, but connecting with your spouse on a deeper level makes the effort worthwhile.

Taking time to unplug from the outside world and plug into our relationships is critical. Especially when life is busy and stressful, that little bit of time together really has to count. "Job stress spills over into our relationships," says Terri Orbuch, a sociologist and director of a long-term study on marriage funded by the National Institutes of Health. "It can be not getting along with our colleagues or our boss . . . or the actual amount of time that we need to spend at work or doing work at home that spills over and affects our marriages negatively," says

Orbuch, author of "5 Simple Steps to Take Your Marriage From Good to Great." [2]

Stepping out of work mode (including work around the house) encourages positive communication, which is why marriage counselors usually recommend date nights. Sadly, we can look around any restaurant and notice how many diners are more engaged with their smart phones than with their companions. The traditional night out to dinner has become pretty lame. Activities requiring cooperation and interaction are better suited to communication and bonding.

Quality Companionship

Talking and emotional expression are critical to marriage, but just *doing* is important, too. As Elvis Presley pointed out, sometime relationships need "a little less conversation and a little more action."

One of the top five needs of married men is "recreational companionship," or shared activity.[4] It makes them feel connected and bonded. Generally, men experience a sense of closeness during shared activity more than they do during conversation. Women are quick to assume that "activity" refers to one in particular, which is important of course, but men enjoy sharing a variety of experiences with their wives. Whether for cultural or biological reasons, men don't connect by talking as women do. They have no need to discuss their lives with their guy friends over the phone. They prefer to discuss matters during, say, a vigorous game of basketball. Friendships are always better between men when they are doing things. This is the way they bond.

Yes, men can and do learn to communicate with their wives, but it requires them to step outside their comfort zones. A woman generally expects a man to relate to her on her terms. Women, if we want to engage with our men in a fresh way, we can step outside our own comfort zones, too. We can go outside, work up a sweat alongside our husbands and see how they respond. Raising our heart rates is refreshing, and when a man feels refreshed, he's more likely to open up. When a man feels relaxed, his walls come down.

Shared activities don't have to be athletic, but sweating together offers some big advantages. For one, exercise is beneficial to health, and who doesn't want a longer, healthier life? Athletic activities also foster competition, and there's nothing like a little healthy competition to spice up a relationship. Another benefit is that adrenaline makes the people around us appear more attractive, so you and your spouse may never look better to each other than when doing something active and exciting together.

An interesting phenomenon is that cyclists ride faster in packs than when solo. When we are part of a community or a team, we are more likely to push ourselves towards improvement. We are accountable for showing up and then keeping up the pace. A team encourages us and recognizes our efforts. As you know, Josh and I view our marriage as a little team, so naturally we believe that these benefits of companionship apply to recreational pursuits. We love being there to encourage each other to climb harder or ride faster.

Some couples have absolutely no interest in sweating together, which is fine. Even so, they need to share activities that are stimulating and engaging, which could include art, music, dance or games.

The Art of Sharing

There was a network TV show on for a couple of seasons called *The Marriage Ref*. On it, a panel of celebrity judges "refereed," or decided whether the husband or the wife was "right," in a marital disagreement. Frequently, the conflict revolved around a hobby or interest enjoyed by one member of the couple. Often, the wife thought that her husband spent too much time on his hobby. He had a fun distraction, but she worried that he wanted or needed to escape her and the marriage. The wife's insecurity prevented her from realizing that her husband didn't see it that way at all. In most instances, he was happy to have her join him in his hobby, but she stubbornly avoided it, certain that she wouldn't have fun. Some women would go so far in justifying their disinterest that they would belittle the activity. Teasing your spouse about something that brings them joy does nothing to build trust in the relationship.

Because the wife would neither join her husband nor develop her own outside interests, she sat at home and pouted about her husband not spending enough time with her or going shopping with her. Neither partner was willing to step out of their own worlds to discover the other's.

Shopping and eating are things we have to do as part of our daily subsistence. Watching TV is something we do to relax and disengage. When it comes to spending quality time together, we need to be a little more creative. The joy of a road trip is discovery. It is a delight to explore new places and sights, like the world's largest frying pan (which can be found in Brandon, Iowa), ball of yarn (Cawker City, Kansas) or ball of rubber bands (Wilmington, Delaware). Marriage is enriched when husbands and wives discover new things together.

The love of activities that Josh and I share has really brought satisfaction to our marriage. Of course, we know that our life together will progress and change, and we understand that we may not always be able to climb rocks and mountain bike. We plan on that, but we have no intention of allowing life changes to alter our shared values. We'll always share a sense of adventure, a zest for life and an appreciation for the outdoors. Later in life, we can take up any number of more "low impact" activities together.

A Storehouse of Shared Memories

Keeping tabs on your spouse throughout the years is always important. It's important to know when they are bored or have stopped enjoying an activity. There is no need to stop learning what makes them tick and what drives them. You can actively encourage yourself to take an interest in the things that interest them and to try new things together. You can encourage your husband or wife to share their dreams and talk about things that they would like to try—giving them a safe place to express any ambition, however unusual or crazy.

Trying new things together may have unexpected benefits. Getting out of our comfort zones can be a great way to unclog lines of communication. When in a new setting, perhaps one that is a bit uncomfortable, we feel vulnerable. We respond to vulnerability by expressing ourselves. Will that expression always be happy and sunny? No, but it will be a guaranteed conversation starter and will probably generate a pretty memorable experience. Good or bad, new experiences generate fresh communication.

Still afraid to try something that your spouse wants to do? Think it might be boring, uncomfortable or even worse? Hesitation about taking risks and trying new things is often a trait that develops at an early age, but it's a characteristic that can be changed. It's a matter of putting some pressure on yourself to step out.

It takes practice to be comfortable with being uncomfortable, so we can start gradually. To set ourselves up for success, we can make sure that the conditions are safe and comfortable. For outdoor activities, we can make sure that the weather forecast is pleasant. We can surround ourselves with people who are patient and encouraging. We can take care to have the right equipment or any special clothing required. Planning and preparation might include spending a little extra money to ensure the best experience possible, but it will be worth it.

Set up for Success

When a new experience doesn't prove to be amazing, it is no cause for discouragement. Being open-minded leaves the door open for trying and enjoying other new things. And just as kids have to try a new food a couple of times to warm up to it, sometimes we have to try an activity a couple of times to get the hang of it. The first time we do something, it can be hard to get past the awkwardness of stepping away from our comfort zones. The second attempt will probably be more relaxed right from the start, setting the stage for a positive experience.

Living in Arizona, the most accessible sports for Josh and me are mountain biking and rock climbing. However, Josh also enjoys surfing and skiing, and he wanted to share those sports with me.

Although I generally enjoy trying new things, surfing and skiing were two activities I was not so excited about. I do not enjoy being cold, so floating around in the chilly waters of the Pacific, and waiting to be pummeled by waves, or flying down a hill of snow with cold wind whipping through my hair were experiences that I thought I could live without. Both activities have pretty steep learning curves, as well. It's pretty likely that new surfers won't be able to stand on their boards on the first day out. Knowing this, I went surfing for the first time, resolved to enjoy it. Seriously. I didn't let myself get whiny, and I didn't give up after hours of failed attempts to catch a wave. Yeah, it was frustrating, but I was on a beautiful beach, playing in the water, and I was determined to embrace the experience and have fun with the challenge.

If a couple is at a loss for an activity that they can enjoy together, an easy place to start is volunteering. No matter how you choose to give, it's hard to feel bad when doing something for others. Helping people is an almost guaranteed way to feel happy. It distracts you from your own problems, needs and stresses, and it often helps you feel more grateful for what you already have. Sharing that positive experience with your husband or wife is almost like doubling the benefit of your time investment.

Nurturing our Joint Spiritual Life

Another activity guaranteed to provide a maximum return on investment is spending time with God together. Ecclesiastes 4:12 tells us that "a cord of three strands is not easily broken" (NIV). God doesn't tell us that the cord can never be broken; he tells us that it is *not easily* broken. Two Christians who are bound together in Christ are stronger together than they are separate. Despite that strength, Matthew 19:6 cautions us not to separate what God has joined together. We know that we can count on God to hold us tight, while we also care for our own strands to prevent them from unraveling.

We are told that "where two or three are gathered together in My name, I am there in the midst of them" (Mt. 18:20), so when we pray with our spouses, we invite the presence of the Lord to be with us powerfully. If the prayers of any two people are powerful, then the prayers of a couple joined by the Lord Himself and united by the Holy Spirit have world-changing potential.

Plenty of long-married couples say that their secret is daily prayer together. Marriage counselor, Rev. Rob Ruhnke says, "I have never talked with a couple whose marriage is coming apart and listened to them tell me that they are praying together each day, but it is not doing any good."[5]

Prayer brings us back to the "oneness" that defines marriage. It is impossible to pray without opening oneself to others. Prayer encourages an attitude of humility, service, listening and caring, making it one of the most powerful ways to unify relationships. We know how important forgiveness is within marriage, and research shows that spouses who pray for each other are more willing to forgive one another's transgressions.[6]

Prayer helps cultivate an attitude of gratitude, which is associated with better mental health and happier relationships. Prayer regulates emotions as well. Praying for and with your spouse provides relaxation, easing the way for day-to-day tensions and conflicts to fade away. [7]

We can nurture our joint spiritual lives in other ways besides praying together. Many couples complete Bible studies together, or they develop their own by reading books or articles, watching movies or listening to messages. They then talk about what they have read or heard, share their responses and discuss what they learned. No matter how a couple chooses to do it, pursuing God together creates deep and lasting bonds.

Summary

Marriage should be more like a fun, scenic drive than a commute to work. We shouldn't feel as though we're clocking in and out, logging enough time to earn the title of husband or wife. We can't engage cruise control and zone out, either, failing to engage, to be present or to appreciate our spouses.

Life doesn't always give us complete control over how much time we spend with our spouses. Fortunately, the quantity of time available to us isn't as important as the quality of the time that we spend with them. When we're together, we want to maximize our time by being fully engaged in interaction. Personal interaction is becoming more difficult in an electronic world, so we may have to intentionally practice communication skills. We have to practice listening, which may mean slowing down or listening to something we've heard before. Even so, connecting on a deeper level is well worth the patience required.

Fortunately, being engaged isn't always about staring into each other's eyes while having long, heartfelt conversations. Full engagement can be plenty active. In fact, recreational companionship is important to a healthy marriage—so get out there and play!

RoadMap for Marriage

Questions for Reflection
1. What activities do you currently enjoy with your spouse? Why do you find them enjoyable?
2. What new activities would you like to try together? What is keeping you from doing so?
3. What can you do together to grow spiritually?

Action Steps
1. Talk to each other about how you spend your time together. Do you spend most of your time passively hanging out, or do you spend it engaged and interested in each other?

CHAPTER 13

BORN TO BE WILD
Live Big

e Harmony's founder, Neil Clark Warren, says that one of the five most common characteristics of lasting love is a belief in "living big."

The future is limitless for two people who are committed to each other. Great lovers not only dare to believe this, they live it. Work together on making your dreams come true. And keep giving yourselves new goals to aim for, new opportunities to grow as a couple. You'll see how true love becomes even more thrilling and stimulating with every leap forward![3]

Aminda and I hadn't read this quote when we embarked on our road trip, but it could have summed up our motivation. We know that as a team we have the potential to be better people and do greater things. To maximize that potential, we consistently practice bringing out the best in each other, which requires being engaged, involved and present in our marriage.

Our road trip wasn't planned on a whim. It was a couple of years in the making. Once we had the idea, we started talking about it. We imagined what we wanted to do, visualized where we wanted to go and figured out what it would take to make it happen. Then we started acting, planning and organizing. It was a fun process, full of shared excitement and anticipation.

It is sad to hear of couples who let their marriages disintegrate and *then* embark on an adventure all alone. Marriage is such an adventure if we let it be. When we experience new places with our spouses, we experience the world not only through our own eyes but through theirs, as well. They point out sights we wouldn't have noticed, and they have insights and knowledge that we don't. There are thousands of places to see and millions of things to do—experiences waiting for each unique couple to share and enjoy together.

Believe for Bigger

Dream big by setting yourself seemingly impossible challenges.
You then have to catch up with them.
— **Richard Branson**[1]

When we feel as though our dreams are out of reach or unattainable, we can't give up on them. Whether we are moving from an apartment to a house, starting a family or advancing a career, we keep dreaming big! God created marriage, and He wants it to be fulfilling. He commanded us to be fruitful and to multiply. We can live out that command in personal, unique ways—having a big house full of kids, creating a business that employs people or engaging in a ministry that touches the world. The form of our fruitfulness doesn't matter, as long as we expect only God's best as we fulfill His commands.

My (Aminda's) high school youth group occasionally played a game called Bigger and Better. We formed teams, each of which was given a single small item like a used pencil or a paper clip. We then scattered ourselves across the neighborhood knocked on doors, presented the item to the people who answered and asked if they had anything they would like to trade. The goal was to make trades that generated something "bigger and better" until we had something that would actually be of value to the group. One year we ended up with a new couch for our meeting room!

In the same way, we should be motivated to seek bigger and better lives. The Word tells us that as we meditate on the glory of the Lord, we ourselves are transfigured, moving from glory to glory, or into increasing levels of distinction or prosperity (Eph. 3:18). He promises that He wants to bless us with "bigger and better" as we keep our gaze focused on Him.

When God gives us desires, we can have faith that He will, in His time, manifest them in reality. We must keep praying and believing, reminding God of His promises and of His faithfulness to grant us the desires of our hearts, always believing that God wants to bless us. We find this truth in the prayer of Jabez. Although Jabez is a very minor character in Bible, his profound one-sentence prayer was important enough to be written. He said, "Bless me indeed and expand my territory." Jabez wasn't afraid to ask for bigger and better, and the last we hear about him are the words, "…and God granted him his request" (I Chron. 4:9-10).

Accept His Best

Many Christians don't feel that they deserve "bigger and better." Instead, they feel unworthy, unprepared, untalented or unskilled. Some may be afraid to dream bigger because they feel as though they don't deserve the good lives they are already living. Their good lives seem fake, and they fear that if their inner selves were exposed, everything would crumble. Married Christians may feel that a spouse is "out of their league," and they may worry that the "superior" spouse will wake up one morning and find a flawed partner on other side of the bed. In the work place, Christians can feel that their good jobs are a result of lucky breaks or reorganization rather than their qualifications or talent.

It is time to accept ourselves just as we are. We know that *all* have sinned and come short of the glory of God. None are worthy, yet our good Father rewards us anyway. We can give thanks for the blessings we have already received, and embrace our destinies by getting out of God's way so that He can continue what he has planned for us.

We don't have to be flashy or famous to "live big." Living big comes from acknowledging that we were created with the ability to do great things—across the world, in our own homes or in our own communities. When we organize a community garden, paint a mural or support a political cause that impassions us, we are expanding our lives. Living big is nothing more than challenging ourselves to make every day count, which simply means spending more time living our own lives than we do watching people on TV. Allowing insecurities to stifle our purposes keeps our lives smaller than they were intended to be. We can step outside our comfort zones and expand our worlds by doing any number of things, like starting a business, earning another degree, learning a new language or just saying hello to a new neighbor.

In his book, *Seven Habits of Highly Effective People,* Stephen Covey explains that we all have concerns which fill our lives, from common ones like work and family to larger ones like global warming and world peace. Together, they create what he calls a person's circle of concern. However, within that circle one has some level of control over only a few of those concerns, and it is these that make up one's circle of influence. When people choose to invest time and energy into that circle of influence, they can control concerns to the extent that they take pro-active steps toward moving life forward. On the other hand, worrying about things over which they have no control just wastes time and energy, and prevents successful forward progress.

Try, Try Again

What do we do when we've read the prayer of Jabez, prayed the prayer, believed for blessing and . . . nothing? How do we muster the faith to see it through? Aminda and I are here to say, "Don't give up!"

Life is full of transitions and phases; times when we feel uncertain about the future. Although we may not be aware of it, God actively uses these times when we can't see ahead or when our current state makes no sense. He may be providing us with a much needed period of restoration, or perhaps He is preparing us for the next big thing. Whether or not we're aware of His purposes during times of uncertainty, we can keep the faith, which is the "substance of things hoped for..." (Heb. 11:1). "Hoped for" means *expected*. Keeping the faith is keeping an attitude of expectation.

In our digital age, life moves fast. We expect things to happen quickly, but God's timeline is different from ours. To Him who is the beginning and the end, our entire lives pass like a blink of an eye, so we can trust that He's not moving too slowly.

When we become discouraged about delayed promises, we can look to the story of Abraham for inspiration. God promised Abraham many descendants, but he didn't have his first son until 25 years later. *Twenty five years.* And no, Abraham wasn't a child when God made that promise; he was already 75 years old! Abraham patiently endured. God had promised him a harvest, and he expected it. It's no wonder that today, thousands of years later, Abraham is still honored as the embodiment of patience and faithfulness.

While Abraham waited for God's promise, he participated in the process of producing an heir. Abraham trusted God to fulfill His part supernaturally, but he didn't wait for an immaculate conception. He did what was physically required. Abraham's story also reveals what happens when we replace participating in God's work with doing His work for Him. Because he and his wife were well past the normal age for child bearing, Abraham faltered in his faith, jumped the gun and attempted to speed up God's work. The result was an out-of-wedlock heir, which was not in God's plan. Even though Abraham had to deal with the consequences of his decision, God didn't let the mistake mess up His good work. Eventually, when he was 100 years old, Abraham and his wife had a son, Isaac, God's promised heir.

Wait for His Way

In portions of the Grand Canyon, Tamarisk trees dominate the landscape along the Colorado River. Imported and planted in the late 1920's to stabilize soil along rivers, huge clusters of them still grow on many of the beaches and in side canyons along the waterway. The Asian Tamarisk tree is not suited to the ecosystem in the Grand Canyon. According to the National Park Service, "the prolific shrub displaces native vegetation and animals. It spreads aggressively, often lowering precious water tables, negatively affecting wildlife and native vegetative communities. For decades, the Park Service has invested time and money…to control the spread of the Tamarisk and to protect other plant species in the Grand Canyon."[2] Whoever sowed the tamarisks was clearly in need of a fast solution or personal recognition for addressing an immediate problem, but failed to carry out the research that would have prevented an expensive, time-consuming harvest in the future.

Without faith and patience, good intentions can go bad. When we try to make things happen unnaturally, we end up with unnatural results. When we take things into our own hands instead of patiently waiting upon the Lord, we hinder His efforts. If we keep believing, keep planning and keep preparing, we will see His promises fulfilled. Our part is to work hard, continuing to use the gifts and talents that He has bestowed upon us, and to leave the miracles to Him. If we faithfully believe His daily promises and do our earthly part to prepare for them, we will spend our lives embracing the "bigger and better" that He has planned for us.

You Only Live Once

We've all heard that "you only live once," usually as an excuse to do something stupid or reckless, but there is some truth in the concept. The idea behind it has been around throughout history, and a more refined version of the saying is "Carpe diem," Latin for "seize the day."

Keeping in mind that we live forever once we leave this earth, we know that our earthly lives zoom by at a rapid pace, so we want to take every opportunity to make our short time here count. One way to do that is to make sure that our lives reflect the values of our Creator, and one of the values He holds most dear is respect for marriage.

The world works hard to convince us that marriage is a boring institution that wasn't meant to last for decades. We can't allow ourselves to be sucked into the world's lie that we have to look outside our marriages to find fun and excitement. We can easily find adventure and exhilaration with our spouses, as long as we are willing to let ourselves be vulnerable. Overcoming fears and risks together can be an awesome bonding experience.

Walking through fear is absolutely liberating. Life offers an endless list of things to be afraid of, and we all develop different ways of coping with them. We all face our own personal challenges, and fear is one of them. It doesn't just go away. We have to walk through it. In one form or another, fear will always be present in our lives, but we don't want it to control us or prevent us from doing amazing things.

When you choose to face fear alongside someone whom you care about, you have two sources of motivation: doing it for your own sense of accomplishment and doing it to strengthen the relationship. When you face your fears in the presence of your partner, you both benefit. Your spouse is psyched and excited to see you succeed. Seeing your spouse push through a challenge generates a deeper level of respect for them, which in turn encourages them to step out and face other fears. It's contagious! The experience of facing challenges and fears together forms a wonderful bond between husbands and wives. In the end, you both feel awesome!

Face-off with Fear

Some of the best memories that Josh and I share are of times when we faced fear together. One time in particular was when I faced my fear of whitewater—rough, cold, wild water. I feared choppy oceans or raging rivers—the possibility of being tossed around like a rag doll in churning waves.

One of my most terrifying moments occurred in a little inflatable kayak, while I was staring into class 4 rapids on the Colorado River in the Grand Canyon. On the previous night I had fallen asleep to the sound of the monstrous current, and now it was time to cross it. I imagined how it would feel to cross that stretch of white water in such a small boat, and all I could think of was being vulnerable and alone, having nothing to rely on but my own strength and capability. I imagined losing control, being thrown out of the boat and being swept away by that cold, churning water.

As scary as it sounds, the truth is that most of my fears were unjustified. I was tagging along with Josh, who was a boat captain for a group of a dozen friends. We spent most of our time in large paddle rafts or oar boats, where we sat comfortably a couple of feet above the water, surrounded by other people. But Josh always brought a couple of inflatable kayaks on river trips, because adventurous participants found them to be lots of fun. I knew that the little boats were wide and stable, and that using them didn't require advanced skills or techniques. During previous days, I had watched several men successfully navigate the river in them. While a couple of those men had "gone swimming," their personal flotation devices brought them right up to the surface, and they floated along until someone could help them back into a boat.

I knew how to paddle and steer a kayak, and I was familiar with the proper position to take if I "went swimming," so there was no logical reason for my stomach being in knots. Paddling in circles around a peaceful little eddy about two hundred yards from the mouth of the rapids, I told myself, "It will be fun, like a roller coaster ride. It's a hot day and being in the water will be refreshing." I was determined to have fun and feel good about facing my fear. I prayed and sang songs to distract myself from feeling terrified and to suppress the scream bubbling up inside.

"Are you sure you want to do this?" called Josh, clearly concerned by the look of terror on my face.

"I'm sure, Babe," I answered as confidently as possible. "I'll always regret not trying it if I don't. I know it will be fun once I get going."

The point of no return finally arrived. As Josh guided the last passenger boat into the flow of water that would carry it through the rapids, I did my best to duplicate its path. Suddenly, there I was. I couldn't see a thing beyond the surrounding walls of water. "Keep paddling, keep paddling," was my mantra, my rhythm. "Oh, no you don't!" I yelled to any wave that threatened to knock me off course, and I punched the paddle down hard into the offending swell. "Keep paddling, keep …." As suddenly as the fury had started, the water became a peaceful flow, pulling me gently down the river to where the other boats were waiting. After I located Josh in the crowd, my first words were, "I want to do it again!" My huge grin made it clear that my fear had been replaced with joy.

Fear exposes our need for control, because facing it requires being uncomfortable with the unknown and a willingness to walk through the discomfort. Fortunately, when we can't see the future, we can always trust the One who does: the Alpha and Omega. We can trust that He will not give us more than we can bear and that He wants only the best for us. With confidence in Him, we should be inspired to step out and seize each day.

Summary

The world works hard to convince us that marriage is a boring institution that wasn't meant to endure. We can't allow ourselves to be deceived by the lie that we have to look outside marriage to find fun and excitement.

Marriage can be an amazing adventure. God created marriage, and He wants it to be fulfilling. We can expect only God's best for us as we seek His ways. If we know that God has given us desires, we can have faith that He will, in his time, fulfill them. Waiting on Him includes planning, preparing and believing. Our part in living the life He has planned for us is to seize each day and step out in faith, knowing that we are meant to look towards the "bigger and better."

RoadMap for Marriage

Questions for Reflection

1. In what ways are you and your partner stronger as partners than as individuals?
2. Are you impatient with God because of unfulfilled dreams in your life? What can you do to nurture those dreams and cultivate an attitude of expectation?
3. Do you have any dreams that are held back by fear?

Action Steps

1. Identify a place that inspires you to think big—maybe the top of a hill or a sky-rise building, a certain store, park, church or community. Commit to spending time there in prayer, receiving God's plan for your future and envisioning it.

2. Identify a big, audacious goal you have for your life. What is the first thing that would have to happen for that goal to be realized? Make a list of actions you can take to achieve that first step, then start checking off the list. Once that is accomplished, move on to the next step, then the next.

ABOUT THE AUTHORS

 Josh is an experienced and passionate educator, having worked as a college professor, a teambuilding facilitator and a volunteer youth counselor. He holds a BS in Psychology and an MS in Adventure Education.

Aminda's articles have been published in outlets including blogs, national ministry newsletters and trade publications. She holds a BA in Communications and an MS in Marketing. They currently reside in Phoenix.

REFERENCES

Chapter 1. Fuel Up:
Inject High Performance Thinking Into Your Marriage

1. Gottman, John M. *The Relationship Cure*, 2001, Crown Publishers, New York

Chapter 2. Keep Your Sparkplugs Clean:
Generating Positive Words and Actions

1. "The Top 7 Ways to Improve Your Marriage," The Gottman Institute, accessed August 13, 2014, http://www.gottman.com/top-7-ways-to-improve-your-marriage/
2. "The 7 Myths of Marriage," *eHarmony*, accessed November 18, 2013, http://www.eharmony.com/dating-advice/relationships/the-7-myths-of-marriage

Chapter 3. Know Your Coordinates:
Keeping Tabs on Your Partner

1. Gottman, John M. *The Relationship Cure*. 2001. Crown Publishers, New York

2. 4 Words to Say to Him Every Day, *Redbook*, accessed November 18, 2013. http://www.redbookmag.com/love-sex/advice/what-to-say-to-your-husband-every-day?click=main_sr

Chapter 4. U-Turns not Allowed:
Stay Committed to the Present

1. Maxwell, John C. *The Maxwell Leadership Bible: New King James Version*. Nashville, TN: Thomas Nelson, 2007. Print.
2. Ibid
3. Janet A Young and Michelle D Pain, "The Zone: Evidence of a Universal Phenomenon for Athletes Across Sports," *Athletic Insight: the Online Journal of Sport Psychology* 1, no. 3 (November 1999): 28, http://www.athleticinsight.com/Vol1Iss3/Empirical_Zone.htm

Chapter 6. Brake Check: Trusting your Life Partner

1. trust. Dictionary.com. Dictionary.com Unabridged. Random House, Inc. http://dictionary.reference.com/browse/trust (accessed: November 22, 2013).
2. Megan Tschannen-Moran, Wayne Hoy, (1998) "Trust in schools: a conceptual and empirical analysis", Journal of Educational Administration, Vol. 36 Iss: 4, pp.334 – 352.
3. Celine Roque, "How to Use Communication to Establish Trust in Remote Teams," February 1, 2011, accessed November 22, 2013. http://gigaom.com/collaboration/how-to-use-communication-to-establish-trust-in-remote-teams/

Chapter 7. Slug bug! Cultivate a Healthy Sense of Humor

1. Gil Greengross, "Laughing All the Way to the Bedroom; The Importance of Humor in Mating," *Psychology Today*, May 1, 2011, accessed November 22, 2011. http://www.psychologytoday.

com/blog/humor-sapiens/201105/laughing-all-the-way-the-bedroom?page=2

2. "Laughter Heals," WebMD video, accessed November 22, 2013. www.webmd.com/balance/video/laughter-heals

3. Gil Greengross, "Laughing All the Way to the Bedroom; The Importance of Humor in Mating," *Psychology Today*, May 1, 2011, accessed November 22, 2011. http://www.psychologytoday.com/blog/humor-sapiens/201105/laughing-all-the-way-the-bedroom?page=2

4. Megan Gibson, "Women Who Use 'Guy Humor' Get All the Guys," Time NewsFeed, May 25, 2011, accessed November 22, 2013. http://newsfeed.time.com/2011/05/25/survey-ladies-who-use-guy-humor-get-all-the-guys/

5. Claire, Kittredge, "The Physical Side of Stress," Everyday Health, accessed November 22, 2013. http://www.everydayhealth.com/womens-health/physical-side-of-stress.aspx

6. Gottman, John M., *The Relationship Cure*. 2001. Crown Publishers, New York.

Chapter 8. There's Only One Driver's Seat: The Importance of Designated Roles

1. Gottman, John M., *The Relationship Cure*. 2001. Crown Publishers, New York.

2. Suzanne Venker, "The War on Men," *Fox News*, November 26, 2012. http://www.foxnews.com/opinion/2012/11/24/war-on-men/

3. Ibid.

Chapter 9. Are We There Yet? Finding Healthy Alone Time

1. Hans Villarica, "How Not to Feel Lonely in a Crowd," *Time*, October 11, 2010, http://healthland.time.com/2010/10/11/how-not-to-feel-lonely-in-a-crowd/

2. Jim Rohn, "The Law of Average," uploaded January 28, 2011. http://www.youtube.com/watch?v=DMmz-MLudQ&feature=player_embedded

3. Stormie Omartian, "How the Power of Prayer Changed my Life," accessed November 18, 2013, http://www.stormieomartian.com/powerofprayer.html

Chapter 10. Fender-benders Happen: The Practice of Forgiveness

1. Dr. Fred Luskin, "Forgiveness 101," *Guideposts*, November 2011.

Chapter 11. Caution, Steep Curves Ahead: Speaking the Truth in Love

1. Deborah Shapiro, "How to Get Along for 500 Days Alone Together," *BBC News Magazine*, March 1, 2013, http://www.bbc.co.uk/news/magazine-21619765

2. Goleman, Daniel. *Emotional Intelligence*. Bantam Books, New York. 1994, p. 60.

3. Ibid, p.170.

4. Stormie Omartian, "How the Power of Prayer Changed my Life," accessed November 18, 2013, http://www.stormieomartian.com/powerofprayer.html

Chapter 12. Taking the Scenic Route: Quality Time Over Quantity

1. Deborah Shapiro, "How to Get Along for 500 Days Alone Together," *BBC News Magazine*, March 1, 2013, http://www.bbc.co.uk/news/magazine-21619765

2. Dr. Terri Orbuch, "How Being Happy at Work Could Improve Your Marital Satisfaction, Too," *The Huffington Post*, May 18, 2011, http://www.huffingtonpost.com/dr-terri-orbuch/job-satisfaction_b_859855.html

3. Ellen McCarthy, "Study Breaks down Divorce Rates by Occupation," *Washington Post*, September 19, 2010, http://www.washingtonpost.com/wp-dyn/content/article/2010/09/16/AR2010091607509.html

4. Neil Clark Warren, "Advice for Love: Think We!," *Guideposts*, accessed November 18, 2013, http://www.guideposts.org/personal-growth/advice-happiness-love

5. Copeland, K., & Copeland, G. *One word from God can change your relationships*. Fort Worth, Tex: Kenneth Copeland Publications, 2000. 32.

6. Rev. Robert A. Ruhnke, "Prayer in Marriage," *For Better and Forever: Marriage Preparation Resources*, accessed August 13, 2014, http://marriagepreparation.com/page/?pg=68

7. Ibid.

8. Ibid.

Chapter 13. Born to be Wild: Live Big

1. Leigh Buchanan, "Richard Branson: 'Screw It. Let's Do It,'" *Inc. Magazine*, Last updated October 31, 2012, http://www.inc.com/magazine/201211/leigh-buchanan/sir-audacity-richard-branson.html

2. "Tamarisk Management and Tributary Restoration," *National Park Service Bulletin*, March 2011. http://www.nps.gov/grca/naturescience/exotic-tamarisk.htm

Printed in the USA
CPSIA information can be obtained
at www.ICGtesting.com
JSHW022344140824
68134JS00019B/1679